Wings *of* Healing

On Faith for Daily Life

J. WILMER GRESHAM

PARACLETE PRESS
BREWSTER, MASSACHUSETTS

Library of Congress Cataloging-in-Publication Data

Wings of healing : on faith for daily life / [notes by] J. Wilmer
Gresham.
    p. cm.
Originally published: San Francisco : Morgan Co., 1927.
    ISBN 1-55725-255-6 (pbk.)
    1. Meditations. I. Gresham, J. Wilmer (James Wilmer), b. 1871.
    BV4801 .W56 2000
    242—dc21   00-009094

Originally published in 1927 by The Morgan Company,
SanFrancisco

10 9 8 7 6 5 4 3 2 1

Published by Paraclete Press
Brewster, Massachusetts
www.paracletepress.com

Printed in the United States of America.

For the Touch of the Healer
of Body and Soul
and Spirit

To all who are strong and seek his consecration,
To all who are spent and seek his renewal,
To all who are suffering and seek his release,
To all who are disheartened and seek his cheer,
To all who are tired and seek his rest,
To all who are adrift and seek his friendship,
To all who are confused and seek his guidance,

this little book is dedicated

PRAYER FOR THE PRESENCE OF CHRIST

O living Christ, make us conscious now of Thy healing nearness. Touch our eyes that we may see Thee; open our ears that we may hear Thy voice; enter our hearts that we may know Thy love. Overshadow our souls and bodies with Thy presence, that we may partake of Thy strength, Thy love and Thy healing life.

HEALING PRAYER OF INTERCESSION

O most gracious and loving Father, purify our souls from everything that may hide Thee from us. Let us feel Thy quickening power flowing through us, building us up in strength and sweetness. Consecrate our talents, our time and our thoughts to Thy holy service. Strengthen us in spirit, in soul, and in body, that we may become living channels of Thy truth and Thy love. Help us to realize that Thou art present with us at all times and in all places, so that we may with perfect faith entrust ourselves and all that are dear to us to Thy never-failing care through Jesus Christ our Lord.

Contents

GOODNESS
All Around Us

COMFORT AND PEACE
from God

COURAGE
for Our Daily Walk

LOVE
to Guide Our Journey

Introduction

In 1910 J. Wilmer Gresham, at the age of thirty-nine, was asked to be the first dean of San Francisco's Grace Cathedral.

It sounded like a prestigious job. A cathedral is, by definition, the principal church in a diocese and the location of the bishop's chair. The dean is the pastor of the cathedral church. If he accepted the job, Gresham could easily become the most influential Episcopal pastor in the state of California. He decided to travel the forty-five miles from his home in San Jose to check out the offer.

THE BEST VIEW IN TOWN

San Francisco in 1910 was full of youthful exuberance. Reduced to rubble and ashes by the great earthquake and fire only four years earlier, the city was back in business with a reformed government, stronger buildings, and plans to become the cultural capital of the West. Grace Cathedral, however, was only an empty lot.

San Francisco's first Episcopal church, the Chapel of Grace, had been founded in 1849 to serve the booming gold rush population. As Grace Church, part way up Nob Hill, it had become the diocesan center. The 1906 earthquake had flattened the church along with everything else in its illustrious neighborhood, including the city's finest mansions at the top of the hill. When the family of railroad baron Charles Crocker surveyed the city block that had been the site of their two fabled homes, they decided to donate the land to the Episcopal Diocese of California. In 1910, then, the first dean of Grace Cathedral would have no church to work in—but he would have the best building site in San Francisco.

Gresham hesitated. He had moved from the South to California for his health. Damp climates were not good for him, and the city by the bay was permeated with chill and fog. Its boundless possibilities, however, called out to his generous nature, and he soon agreed to come.

THE GIFT OF HEALING

Thus began the nearly thirty-year tenure of J. Wilmer Gresham as dean of Grace Cathedral, most of those years in temporary quarters as the magnificent church was being built. Such prolonged camping might have distressed a more worldly man, but Gresham's focus was intensely spiritual. Cathedral archivist Michael D. Lampen characterizes him as "the mystic dean."

"Mystic" is not a word usually applied to the Episcopalians of early twentieth-century America. They were more likely to be leaders of government and industry, powerful pragmatists attracted to Anglican traditionalism and formality. Gresham, born and bred Episcopalian, loved the church's heritage. But "his own religious faith," according to a bishop who worked with him, "lay deep down below the outward customs and their ceremonies which to so many Christians make up the main part of their religion."

One of Gresham's life goals was to foster healing of both soul and body. In the 1920s the cathedral hosted a healing mission for bishops, clergy, physicians, and laypeople of the diocese. Intercessory prayer circles formed, and numerous people reported answers to prayer. Some of Gresham's associates came to believe that the dean had the spiritual charism of healing mentioned by St. Paul (1 Corinthians 12:9), for miraculous healings followed his prayers.

Participants began publishing a weekly newsletter, "The Healing Messenger," to extend the mission's work through inspirational readings on various aspects of the healthy Christian life. In 1927 an editorial committee published selected readings from "The Healing Messenger," along with commentary by Dean Gresham, in book form as *Wings of Healing*. The book proved immensely popular: In fifty years it was printed twenty times, frequently with new material added.

A LEGACY OF LOVE

In the words of Bishop Edward L. Parsons, Gresham's superior for the first half of his time at Grace Cathedral, Dean Gresham converted "a paper organization into a living organism." A major contribution, of course, was his pastoral care during the building of the cathedral itself, a project underway during all twenty-nine of his years as dean. His memory lingers in the carillon bells, which bear inscriptions he chose, as well as in the name of Gresham Hall. In addition, Gresham commissioned the Twenty-Third Psalm window in the south transept in honor of his wife, Emily Cooke Gresham.

But the mystic dean's most enduring legacies are not monuments but memories. Typical is the story of the Jewish businessman who came to Gresham in desperation. His business was about to fail, and he needed five hundred dollars immediately. Gresham, who had never seen the man before, trustingly wrote out a check. Not many days later, the man returned with the five hundred dollars plus interest.

Some years later, Gresham had a heart attack while walking down Market Street. The police, assuming he was drunk, were about to haul him away in the paddy wagon when the businessman happened to walk by. He recognized his benefactor, identified him to the police, and persuaded them to take him to a hospital where his health was restored.

Throughout his life, Gresham consistently and unsparingly helped people in need. Healing the broken was his gift and his calling, his charism and his vocation. It was not possible to be too generous. When a friend scolded him for giving away too much, he responded, "God will take care of me."

And God did take care of him. In spite of his momentary fears in 1910 that the San Francisco fog would ruin his health, Gresham continued as dean until 1939 and ministered as dean emeritus until his death in 1958 at age 87. In a note on the meaning of intercession, Dean Gresham could be summing up his own life and ministry:

"Being the instruments of God's life-communication to others, we ourselves—quite unconsciously—are changed into the image of the divine Intercessor, the Master in the school of prayer. We learn the highest meaning of sharing, the sharing of His ministry of healing and of help."

WINGS OF HEALING

This twenty-first edition of *Wings of Healing* is based on the 1957 printing, the last in Dean Gresham's lifetime, containing his final revisions. It includes nearly a hundred readings, each paired with a note by Gresham.

This is a book to read slowly, perhaps just one selection each morning. The poems and essays, many from the nineteenth century, may evoke nostalgia or even amazement at the seemingly simple faith of an earlier era. But do not romanticize them: Their courage and cheerfulness are hard won. Their authors knew illness and death, poverty and disaster, to an extent nearly forgotten in America today;

Dean Gresham himself, devastated by his wife's death the year after he retired, returned many evenings to the sidewalk in front of their former home, where he was seen silently weeping. But the stained-glass window he commissioned in her honor affirms that the Lord is our shepherd, and that goodness and mercy follow us all the days of our life.

It is the Publishers' hope that readers will continue to be inspired by Dean Gresham's gentle and generous spirit, by his intimacy with and unshakable trust in his Lord, and by his dedication to making the broken whole.

—*LaVonne Neff*
Wheaton, IL
March, 2000

Healing the Broken
(Introductory Note)

There are broken bodies and broken hearts, broken homes, a broken Church, and a broken world. The Master is working in the broad human field to make broken things whole. *The miracle of healing the broken* happens whenever through faith, and the sharing of God's plan, the energies of the divine life are liberated.

To you who read this book the Master says, in his very words of long ago, "Be thou made whole." And then he adds, "I make thee whole *not for thyself* alone, but to have thee *close to Me* in My ministry to the broken everywhere.

"He took the broken fragments of his dreams,
  Such scattered shreds as others toss aside,
And with them wrought another dream so fair
    That others made his dream their faith and
guide."

GOODNESS
All Around Us

That I may know Him. —Philippians 3:10.

Two Ways of Knowing

A professor of speech, on vacation in the highlands, visited a prayer-meeting in a Scotch kirk. During the evening he was asked to read the twenty-third psalm, David's tender psalm of the shepherd, beginning

The Lord is my shepherd, I shall not want;
He maketh me to lie down in green pastures;
He leadeth me beside the still waters.

He read the lines eloquently, with the insight of a rare cultivation in the arts of diction. The congregation was moved by his gifted rendering of the age-old hymn of the shepherd.

The minister of the kirk, a quiet man of more than seventy years, was then asked to read the same psalm. He spoke the words in a soft ancient voice, without effort, without polish, as he had done many a Sunday. As he read, heads were bowed as if in silent prayer and not an eye in the congregation was dry.

When the professor of speech was asked how it happened that when he read the psalm the congregation was moved by his eloquence, but when the minister read it they were moved to tears, he replied:

"The difference is that I *know the psalm*, but the old *minister knows the shepherd.*"

NOTE ON TWO WAYS OF KNOWING

In this precious story of "the prayer-meeting in the kirk" the professor is at least honest with himself. He

2

does not claim to *know the Shepherd*. He only *knows the psalm*. There are many like him. They know their Bibles, recite their creeds, give generously, serve devotedly, even at times receive the tokens of their Lord's broken body and poured out blood. But they know in their hearts and—if they had the professor's courage would confess that their religious life touches only the *forms* of spiritual experience. Not for them is the thrill of the quickening power that flows from the Shepherd of the souls of men, the Shepherd who is forever at their side, though they know him not.

Then there are those who, like the quiet minister of the kirk, *know the Shepherd*. To them he is not a figure framed in articles of religion or frozen in a creed. He is a Person, the most real Person in the world. In his heart is their welfare, their destiny. His dream is to make them like himself. He says to all who will hear his voice, "You are not a mere offspring of nature. You are a child of God. You can incarnate the Christ in the temple of your personality. I am here to show you the way; indeed *I am the way*, for I am the first-born of many brethren.

We first know Christ from without, *objectively*. Thus Paul first knew him when he saw his form, felt his presence, heard his voice on that unforgettable day on the road to Damascus. But there comes to the soul the great moment when he is known *within*. Such a moment came to Paul when the high noon of the road to Damascus softened into the sunset glow of his later years. Then, then only, could he write, "When it pleased God who separated me from my mother's womb and called me by his grace "to reveal his Son *in me*." That experience became the *dividing-line* in his spiritual history. It may become the dividing-line in yours also.

Wanting and Wanting

I don't see how you stand it, God,
Looking right down into men's hearts
All the time.
And seeing them always wanting things
They can't get.
Not things—that's not what I mean—
But what a man or a woman
Wants in his heart:
A chance to do his bit in his own way,
A little time to look up at the sky
And watch the high clouds sailing by,
You know!
And somebody to love, maybe a child,
And a God he feels dead sure about.
Maybe you don't know what it's like
To want and want and want
Up in Heaven with all the angels there,
Unless—perhaps—
I wonder
God! Do you happen to want us?
Well, if you do,
It somehow makes our wanting
Not so hard to stand.
And if you do,
Then we're glad—
For most of all we want You.

There are those who *pray to God* in patterned *forms* of prayer, forms hallowed by memory and association. And there are those who know no formal words of prayer, who scarcely seem to pray at all, but who have learned simply to *talk with God*, as a child to a Father in Heaven, as a man talks with his friend.

It is in this spirit that the accompanying lines were written. The writer voices a heart-hunger and wonders whether God, too, may not be hungry in His heart of hearts. "I don't see how you stand it, God, looking right down into men's hearts all the time, and seeing them always wanting things they cannot get. Maybe you don't know what it's like to *want* and *want* and *want*. Unless, perhaps—I wonder God—do you happen to want *us*? Well, if you do, somehow it makes our wanting not so hard to stand. For *most of all we want You.*"

This prayer-conversation suggests *frustration*, human and divine. William Herbert Carruth has caught the human side of it in his lines:

Like tides on a crescent sea-beach,
      When the moon is new and thin,
Into our hearts high yearnings
      Come welling and surging in
Come from the mystic ocean
      Whose rim no foot has trod,
Some of us call it Longing,
      And others call it God.

But God wants *us* more than we want *him*. He is forever seeking us, waiting for us, waiting for the day when he shall hold us as close to his bosom as he holds the eternal Christ, through whom he would woo us to his Heart of Love.

We look not at the things which are seen, but at the things which are not seen, for the things which are seen are temporal, but the things which are not seen are eternal. —2 Cor. 4:18

Looking Through the Lens

What is Reality? Reality, in the eyes of the practical man, is made up of cold, hard facts. And what are the cold, hard facts of life?

As we look about us we see quarrels, bickerings, unhappiness, unfaithfulness, treachery, covetousness—materialism everywhere. These are the *facts* of life.

But what are facts? Fact comes from *factum*. something that we do or *make*.

But Reality is not what is *made*, but what eternally *is*. Love *is*. Quarrels are *made*. Joy *is*. Unhappiness is *made*. Truth *is*. Lies are *made*. Loyalty *is*. Betrayals are *made*. Life *is*. Sickness is *made*.

Jesus went through life seeing no quarrels, no unhappiness, no lies, no sickness. He looked through earth-made fact and saw eternal reality. *Looking through the Lens* of divine understanding, He saw men and women *whole*. Seeing them *whole*, He brought divine laws and forces into operation, and *hard, ugly facts* were dissolved by *Reality*. This was His method. He bids us master it, promising that the works that He did shall we do also.

—*Glenn Clark*

In the Laboratories of Science man and women are quietly putting their questions to Nature and leading the way to happier living and a better world-order. And in the Laboratories of the Soul there are Seekers after Reality who are recording their findings under the guidance of the Great Technician of life and destiny.

It has been said that we might as well *recognize* the facts of life because, after all is said, we must *live with them*. They exist. They are not delusions of "mortal mind." But it is well to bear in mind that we and the generations back of us have made the *facts*—certainly the *ugly facts*—of life.

But looking at the facts of existence *through the lens of divine understanding* we behold a Spiritual Order, which is perfect as the Father in Heaven is perfect, and which alone can dissolve or transform all that is evil and false and ugly into the good, the true, the beautiful of the Kingdom of Reality. With the Lens of Divine Understanding we look not at the things which are seen but at the things which are not seen, for the things which are seen are temporal, but the things which are not seen are eternal.

Our light affliction, which is but for a moment, worketh for us a far more exceeding and eternal weight of glory. —2 Cor. 4:17

Take Away Pain

The cry of man's anguish went up to God:
  "Lord, take away pain—
The shadow that darkens the world thou hast
      made,
    The close, coiling chain

That strangles the heart; the burden that weighs
    On wings that would soar.
Lord, take away pain from the world Thou hast
      made—
    That it may love Thee the more."

Then answered the Lord to the cry of the world:
    "Shall I take away pain
And with it the power of the soul to endure,
    Made strong by the strain?

Shall I take away pity that knits heart to heart,
    And sacrifice high?
Will you lose all your heroes that lift from the fire
    White brows to the sky?

Shall I take away love that redeems at a price
    And smiles at its loss?
Can ye spare from the lives that would climb
      unto mine
    The Christ on His Cross?"

Many years ago Dr. Horace Bushnell wrote a searching volume on "The Moral Uses of Dark Things."

By "dark things" he meant trouble, misfortune, sorrow, bereavement, death—all the events, all the circumstances, that fling their shadow across the landscape of human existence.

By the "moral uses" of dark things he meant the spiritual values that may be extracted from them. As in physics common clay becomes the ever-changing opal, rough sand the beautiful sapphire, black soot the sparkling diamond.

Shakespeare in "As You Like It" makes his actor say, "Sweet are the *uses* of adversity." He does not say "sweet is adversity." No one can ever think of adversity as sweet. He says "sweet are the *uses* of adversity." That is, priceless are the values that can be extracted from adversity, if we know the secret.

Dark things are more than tests of our powers. They are possible additions to our resources. We drink the blood of our crosses and are vitalized by the pain we defeat. By quiet patience, by strong fighting, by persistent praying, we may suck the innermost secret strength, the very fiber of life itself, out of the dark things that challenge us. We climb the steep ascent of heaven through peril, toil, and pain.

Then I thought to understand this, but it was too painful for me; until I went into the sanctuary of God; then understood I.—Psalm 73:16-17

The Art of Meditation

Meditation is often confused with *reverie*, when the soul is absent and dreaming, and minutes and hours slip by unnoticed under the spell of *fancy*. It is easy to indulge this form of relaxation, but let no one confuse it with Meditation.

Meditation is partly a passive, partly an active state. Whoever has pondered long over a plan which he is anxious to accomplish, without distinctly seeing at first the way, knows what Meditation is.

It is in this way that one of the greatest of English engineers, a man unaccustomed to regular discipline of mind, is said to have accomplished his most marvelous triumphs.

He threw bridges over almost impracticable torrents. He pierced the eternal mountains for his viaducts. Sometimes a difficulty brought all the work to a pause. Then he would shut himself up in his room, eat nothing, speak to no one, abandon himself intensely to the contemplation of that on which his heart was set. And at the end of two or three days, he would come forth serene and calm, walk to the spot, and quietly give orders which seemed the result of superhuman intuition.

Meditation is done in silence. Only in the sacredness of inward silence does the soul meet the secret, hiding God. The strength of resolve, which afterwards shapes life and mixes itself with action, is the fruit of these sacred, solitary moments. There is a divine depth in silence, when in Meditation we meet God alone.

—*Frederick W. Robertson.*

NOTE ON THE ART OF MEDITATION

We have entitled the reading "The Art of Meditation." But meditation is as truly a science as an art. Certain well-defined laws control it. Certain principles determine its effectiveness. Among these is *concentration*, which means literally "drawing to a center." Or, to use another word, the focusing of thought and energy toward a desired end. William Walker points out that when we have learned to concentrate or focus the mind, the next step is to learn the knack of *holding the focus steadily*.

"The sun-glass, if held by a wavering, shaking hand which changes its position constantly, will never *manifest heat*. The sharp-edged tool will accomplish nothing, in spite of its keenness, unless it is held firmly to its task. The *will must be used*, not only in drawing one's energy to a focus, but equally firmly in the work of holding the focused energy steadily upon the task before it.

"This principle of *mental focus* manifests itself strongly in the lives of the great men of the race. It imparts that dynamic 'something' which sweeps away obstacles, and forces itself through insuperable difficulties in the path of achievement."

One thing have I desired of the Lord, even that I may dwell in the house of the Lord, to behold the fair beauty of the Lord, and to visit his temple. —Psalm 27:4

The Beauty of Holiness

Sitting in Lincoln Cathedral, and gazing at one of the loveliest of human works—as the Angel Choir has been described—there arose within me, obliterating for the moment the thousand heraldries and twilight saints and dim emblazonings, a strong sense of reverence for the minds which had executed such things of beauty.

What manner of men were they who could, in those dark days, build such transcendent monuments? What was the secret of their art? By what spirit were they moved?

Absorbed in thought, I did not hear the beginning of the music, and then, as a response to my reverie—and arousing me from it—rang out the clear voice of the boy leading the antiphon, "That thy power, thy glory, and the mightiness of thy kingdom might be known unto men." Here was the answer.

Moving in a world not realized, these men sought, however feebly, to express in glorious structures their conception of the *beauty of holiness*, and these works—our wonder—are but the outward and visible signs of the ideals which animated them.

Practically to us life offers the same problems. Still the ideal State, the ideal Life, the ideal Church—what they are and how best to realize them—such dreams continue to haunt the minds of men, and who can doubt that their contemplation immensely fosters the upward progress of the race?

—*Sir William Osler*

NOTE ON THE BEAUTY OF HOLINESS

It has been said that *life is lived* in *supreme* moments. Moments of *thought*, when our spirits are touched by high inspirations, and we seem to "think God's thoughts after Him." Moments of *emotion*, when aspirations leap like angels from the altar of our hearts. Moments of *action*, when we feel our wills to be one with God's will, and great duties are before us and great songs.

Some such high moment came to William Osler as he sat musing in the hush of a great Cathedral. It came after the silence was broken by a silver thread of music, the music of a boy's voice echoing through the pillared spaces.

To a truly great soul it is but a single step to pass from the "holiness of beauty" to the *beauty* of *holiness*. When Sir William awakens from his reverie he asks himself "by what spirit those men of a bygone age were moved that they should build such transcendent monuments?"—and the answer comes not from himself but from the young singer of the antiphon, "That thy power, thy glory, and the mightiness of thy kingdom might be known to men!" In a word, to manifest the character, the beauty, and the eternal glory of God.

When thou saidst, "Seek ye my face," my heart said unto thee,
"Thy face, Lord, will I seek." —Psalm 27:8

A Shrine of Quietness

Make in my heart a quiet place
And come and dwell therein;
A little shrine of quietness
All sacred to Thyself—

A little place of mystic grace
Of self and sin swept bare,
Where I may look into Thy face
And talk with Thee in prayer.

Come, occupy my silent place
And make Thy dwelling there.
More grace is wrought in quietness
Than any is aware.

—JOHN OXENHAM

"Where I may look into Thy face and talk with Thee in prayer." Here is the heart of John Oxenham's little prayer-poem. How may we look into the Master's face? We are indebted to *Forward* for this story from an old Spanish church.

In an old Spanish church there is a statue of Christ which stands alone in its uniqueness and beauty. Should you travel from afar to see this statue, your disappointment as you first look at it would be great. It is quite ordinary. Then, out of the shadows would come the verger to tell you that the artist so made it *that only those who kneel before it* could see the beauty of the face. You would *kneel* and you would see.

No one knows the beauty of his face until, throwing away all pride, he has come and knelt in wonder and in love, in humility and in repentance, seeking forgiveness.

And then, again, a deeper thought. If the vision of Christ can be seen in a rare statue, may it not be that someone is meant to catch a vision of him from *your* face, even from *you*?"

Verily I say unto you, Wheresoever this gospel shall be preached throughout the whole world, this also that this woman hath done shall be told for a memorial of her. —St. Mark 14:9

The Alabaster Vase

Do not keep the alabaster boxes of your love and sympathy sealed up until your friends are dead. Fill their lives with sweetness. Speak approving, cheering words, while their ears can hear them, and while their hearts can be thrilled and made happier by them. The kind things you mean to say when they are gone say before they go. The flowers you mean to send for their coffins send to brighten and sweeten their homes before they leave them.

If my friends have alabaster boxes full of the fragrant perfumes of love and sympathy which they intend to break over my dead body, I would rather they brought them out in my wearied and troubled moments that I might be cheered and refreshed by them while I need them. I would rather have a plain coffin without a flower, a funeral without a eulogy, than a life without the sweetness of love and sympathy.

Let us learn to anoint our friends *beforehand* for their burial. *Post-mortem kindness* does not cheer the burdened spirit. Flowers on the coffin cast no fragrance backward over the weary way.

NOTE ON THE ALABASTER VASE

The finest acts of life are spontaneous. Just as Shelley wrote the Skylark as freely as the bird itself sings from the cloud; just as Mozart's music flowed from his mind as wind makes music among the branches; just as Turner's pictures sprang out of his brain as a rainbow springs out of a shower so Mary's act came from the depth of her soul.

It was at Bethany. They were all at dinner in Simon's house the Saturday night before the crucifixion. Jesus was the guest of honor, and Lazarus was present—whom he had raised from the dead.

And Mary was there in the presence of her beloved and rescued brother. She sat and thought and gazed—until "the fire burned." She would give some outward align of her love, her gratitude, her adoration. And so she arose, fetched an alabaster vase of Indian spikenard, and came softly behind Jesus where he sat. Then she broke the fragile vase in her hands, and poured the precious perfume, first over his head, then over his feet. And then, unconscious of every presence save his alone, she wiped those feet with the long tresses of her hair, while the atmosphere of the whole house was filled with the delicious fragrance.

Then said Judas Iscariot, "Why was this waste of the ointment made? It might have been sold for more than fifty dollars and given to the poor."

But the Master said, "Let her alone; for in that she hath poured this ointment on my body, she did it for my burial. Verily I say unto you, Wheresoever this gospel shall be preached throughout the whole world, this also, that this woman hath done, shall be told for a memorial of her."

The odor of the ointment filled the festal room. The fragrance of the story, with its immortal beauty and compelling pathos, has been wafted down the Christian centuries, wherever the feet of the messengers of the Prince of Peace have touched.

The Road in the Sky

The woods were dark, and the night was black,
    And only an owl could see the track;
Yet the cheery driver made his way
    Through the great pine woods as if 'twere day.

I asked him, "How do you manage to see?
    The road and the forest are one to me."
"To me as well," he replied, "and I
    Can only drive by the road in the sky."

I looked above, where the branches tall
    Rose from the road like an ebon wall,
And lo! a radiant starry lane
    Wound with the road and made it plain.

And since, when the path of life is drear,
    And all is blackness and doubt and fear,
When shadows darken the scene below
    And I see not a step of the way to go,
Then, ah! then, I look on high
And walk on earth by the *road in the sky*.

NOTE ON THE ROAD IN THE SKY

The cheery driver could not *always* see the Road in the
sky. Sometimes the skies were overcast—as dark as the
ebon woods. *Then* he had to *feel his way* or trust to the
instincts of his faithful animal as he jogged along.

But always there is a Road in the Sky for the seeker

after God. Guide posts may be invisible, landmarks indistinguishable. But the Road is there—if we will but look up.

To a great soul in the stress of doubt there came suddenly the question, "Is there no truth that I believe?" Yes, there is a *distinction of right and wrong* that I have never doubted, and I see not how I can. Have I taken the principle of *right* as my law? I have done *right things*, but have I ever thrown my life out on the principle to become all that *right* requires of me? No, I have not. Then, here is something for me to do. Here I will begin. If there is a God; if He is a *right* God; if I have lost Him in wrong—then I shall find Him in *right*.

Then the decisive moment came. He prayed to the God so dimly seen and felt, asking help that he might begin a *right* life. Then he says:

"As I prayed I chose that *right* thenceforth should be my unalterable, eternal endeavor. I rose from my knees. The whole sky was luminous about me. It was the morning of a new eternity."

Right has become *personal* to us in Christ. He is the Way, as he said. He is the Road in the Sky. We may not believe all that the churches and all that the creeds have said about him. But we can believe *him*—and follow *him*.

> *"If Jesus Christ is a man,—*
> *And only a man,—I say*
> *That of all mankind I cleave to him,*
> *And to him will I cleave alway.*
> *If Jesus Christ is a God,—*
> *And the only God,—I swear*
> *I will follow, Him through heaven and hell,*
> *The earth, the sea, and the air."*

If I go to prepare a place for you I will come again, and receive you unto myself; that where I am ye also may be. —St. John 14:3

The Horizon

*D*eath is only a horizon, and a horizon is but the limit of our sight. What do we mean when we say that death is only a horizon? Is it not something like this?

"You are standing upon the seashore. A ship at your side spreads her white sails or steams out to the morning breeze and starts for the blue ocean.

"She is an object of beauty and strength, and you stand and watch her until at length she hangs like a speck of white cloud just where the sea and sky come down to mingle with each other.

"Then someone at your side says, 'there, she's *gone!*' Gone *where*? Gone *from your sight*—that is all.

"She is just as large in mast and hull and spar as she was when she left your side. Just as able to bear her load of living freight to the place of destination.

"Her diminished size is in you, not in her. And just at the moment when someone at your side says, '*there, she's gone!*' there are other eyes watching her coming, and other voices ready to take up the glad shout, '*there she comes!*'"

That is what we mean when we say that Death is only a horizon.

NOTE ON THE HORIZON
We have not been able to trace the authorship of the accompanying reading, which we have ventured to entitle "The Horizon." In the appended prayer are

found the significant lines "death is only a horizon, and a horizon is nothing but the limit of our sight."

On page 111 will be found the background of the Master's revelation of immortality. The souls of the righteous are in the midst of God "as the islands that slumber in the sea," forever seeking to manifest their presences to consciousness.

"More present to faith's vision keen
Than any other vision seen;
More new, more intimately nigh
Than any other human tie."

The Communion of Saints is not only that which *shall* be. It is that which *now* exists. All whom we have loved, and all who loved us, are ever near because ever in his presence in whom we live and dwell.

A PRAYER

"We seem to give him back to Thee, dear God, who gavest him to us. Yet, as Thou didst not lose him in giving, so we have not lost him by his return to Thee.

"Not as The world givest, givest Thou, O lover of souls. What Thou givest Thou takest not away. For what is Thine is ours always if we are Thine.

"And life is eternal; and love is immortal; and death is only a horizon; and a horizon is nothing save the limit of our sight.

"Lift us up, strong Son of God, that we may see further. Cleanse our eyes, that we may see more clearly. Draw us closer to Thyself that we way know ourselves nearer to our beloved who are with Thee.

"And while Thou dost prepare a place for us, prepare us for that happy place, that where they are and Thou art we too may be."

*They went through the towns, preaching the gospel
and healing everywhere.* —St. Luke 9:6

Spiritual Healing

He who waves away the healing power of Christ as belonging only to early New Testament times is not preaching the whole Gospel. God is not the last resort in sickness. He is the first.

What we need to realize is that not our physical but our spiritual nature is the dominant part of us. It is the monarch that holds sway over the rest of us.

Psychological healing, as it were, goes half way. Spiritual healing goes the whole way and all the way. And it goes hand in hand with all true science. Spiritual healing through prayer is based on as immutable laws of the universe as is electricity or the radio or the airplane.

But we should never overlook the fact that the chief end of religion is that we may know God, from Whom all health and healing come.

—CHARLES H. BRENT

Someone asks: "Why should we not recapture the 'first fine careless rapture' of the early Church? We have the same reasons to rejoice; the same powers at our disposal."

To answer this question is to go right to the heart of the Christian religion. We shall not recapture "the first fine careless rapture" of the Christian religion until we rediscover Christ for ourselves in the totality of his revelation to *our personal lives.* Discovering him for ourselves, we can bear him rapturously to others. Then— and only then—can we interpret him to the social order. It is folly to preach Christ as a panacea for the distress and perplexity of the world *until and unless* we have proved for ourselves his power and mission to *recover the individual.*

Starting with the individual, when the Master said to men and women, "Be ye made whole," he had in view *the healing of soul and body.* The *gospel within the gospel* was the astounding good news that salvation means *health,* and holiness means *wholeness.* It is nothing less than the rebirth of personality. The early Church, that is the *earliest* Church, was a community of reborn personalities.

Professor Jacks speaks of the "lost radiance of the Christian religion." Radiance began to fade from Christianity when this first thing became secondary. Those *who had not been made whole* offered elaborate worship instead, or busied themselves about what they presumed to call *service,* or made a fetish of their frozen *orthodoxies.*

Let us take this first note as our *keynote.* St. Paul has summed it all up in his little prayer, "May your whole person, the spirit and the soul and the body, be preserved blameless in the presence of our Lord Jesus Christ."

He that seeketh findeth. —*St. Matthew 7-8*

The Search

There are so many ways of seeking strength;
 The old, old one of prayer—a slow, still
Ingathering of forces through the length
 Of travelled roads to fortify the will;

The bracing power of music and of song;
 The long, deep look into a loved one's eyes;
The touch of fellow-humans; and along
 Some road the benediction of the skies;

The inspiration of the printed word;
 Color and form; within the heart, alone,
Memory of a voice no longer heard;
 Attunement with all nature's undertone.

Yet, how few see!—the roads are much the
  same—
God moves on each, they vary but in name.

—ANNA HAMILTON WOOD

There is a precious passage in the Confessions of St. Augustine that has touched the world's heart: "Thou hast made us for thyself, O Lord, and our hearts will find no rest till they rest in thee." Like almost every other immortal saying, it is familiar because its music has drifted down the ages. It tells the epic story of our search for God. It is true, deeply and eternally true. But there is a companion truth to which it is indissolubly wedded. God also is searching for us. May we not almost say *that his heart* is restless till we rest in him?

Anna Hamilton Wood points to the *converging lines* that meet at the end of the search. The old, old way of prayer; the threaded line of music and of song; the sacrament of friendship and of love; the ministry of nature and the printed word; the memory of those whom we have loved long since and lost awhile.

The movement of the Eternal may be traced on each ascending line. And they all converge in God, *in God who is our Home*, as Wordsworth said.

These things have I spoken unto you, that my joy might remain in you, and that your joy might be full. —St. John 15:11

Christ A Diffuser of Joy

Christ was a diffuser of joy. That, of course, is the profoundest reason why men and women loved to be with him. The joy which he possessed himself was imparted to all who came in contact with him. "He let the sunshine through."

What was it that made him so joyful? There is one phrase which tells us a part of the secret, the phrase in which he says, "I am not alone, because the Father is with me." He never faced life alone, because he was always conscious of the Presence of God his Father.

Christ faced life in the companionship of God. He carried all burdens, he determined all questions, he faced all problems with the Father as his companion.

The other secret of our Lord's joy is that he lost himself in love and service for those about him. That was the other outstanding characteristic in his life.

The Master's earlier teaching stressed *happiness*. There were eight beatitudes. Each note in that divine octave vibrated to the harmonies of *happiness*. But later in his widening ministry, when the shadows of suffering and of pain gathered round him, he dwelt on *joy*. And it was by a like transition that he passed from his great word *rest* to his greater word *peace*.

The reading portrays Christ as a diffuser *of joy*. He diffused joy as a flower diffuses perfume, as a star diffuses light. But Christ not only *diffused* joy; he *imparted* joy. Out of the silent, unseen world about us he still imparts joy. This joy is always deepest when our mortal life is darkest. It was so with him. Under the very shadow of the Cross he said, "These things have I spoken unto you that my joy might remain in you and that your joy might be full." If momentarily in pain or grief we seem to lose that Joyous Presence, his words come echoing back, "I will see you again, and your heart shall rejoice, and your joy no man taketh from you."

It was Jean Ingelow who wrote:

"It is a comely fashion to be glad
Joy is the grace we say to God."

*I waited patiently for the Lord, and he inclined unto
me and heard my calling.* —Psalm 40:1

The Time Element in Prayer

It takes God time to answer prayer. It takes time for God to make bread from wheat fields. He takes the earth. He pulverizes. He softens. He enriches. He wets with showers and dews. He warms with life. He gives the blade, the stock, the amber grain, and then at last the bread for the hungry. All this takes time. Therefore, we sow, and till, and wait, and trust, until all God's purpose has been wrought out. It takes God time to answer prayer.

*"Back of the loaf is the snowy flour,
    And back of the flour the mill;
And back of the mill is the wheat, and the shower.
    And the sun, and the Father's will."*

There are no unanswered prayers. Sometimes God gives us what we *need* rather than what we *want*. To put it differently, he gives us what we *need* instead of what we *think we want*. But always the response of the Eternal waits at the threshold of our asking and vibrates to every pulsation of our *most real* need.

This reading on "the time element in prayer" brings this *postponed* element into view. We must wait in God's presence as the angels wait around the throne. Patience must have her perfect work. Why? Never to disappoint us, but only to meet our deepest need. "That we may be perfect and entire, wanting nothing." Patience is but another word for faith, and faith means that God will keep faith with Himself as a prayer-answering as well as a prayer-hearing God.

> "Plant patience in the garden of thy soul;
> Its roots are bitter, but its fruit is sweet.
> Beneath its tender shade the burning heat
> And burden of the day shall lose control.
> Plant patience in the garden of thy soul."

I can do all things in Him that strengtheneth me.
—Phil. 4:13

Affirmations of the Spirit

Let me be so strong that nothing can disturb my peace of mind.

Let me look on the sunny side of everything, and make my optimism come true.

Let me think only of the best, work only for the best, and, expect only the best.

Let me be just as enthusiastic about the success of others as I am about my own.

Let me forget the mistakes of the past, and press on to the greater achievements of the future.

Let me wear a cheerful countenance at all times, and have a smile ready for every living creature I meet.

Let me give so much time to the improvement of myself that I shall have no time to criticize others.

Let me be too large for worry, too noble for anger, too strong for fear, and too happy to permit the presence of trouble.

Let me live in the faith that the world is on my side as long as I am true to the best that is in me.

Affirmations are guideposts on the path of healing. They point the way. They also mark the destination, which is health of soul and body.

The perfect affirmation, "I can do all things in him that strengtheneth me," rests upon a consciousness of the indwelling Christ.

This underlies all other affirmations. It weaves the spirit of the Master into the texture of the soul.

When this principle is active, love becomes the law of the heart, truth the law of the mind, obedience the law of the will, life abundant the law of the body.

Affirming our fellowship with Christ in God, we are transformed into the likeness of the Master. We enter the radiant circle of His friends.

The Things that Count

Not what we have, but what we use;
Not what we see, but what we choose—
These are the things that mar or bless
The sum of human happiness.

The things near by, not things afar;
Not what we seem, but what we are—
These are the things that make or break,
That give the heart its joy or ache.

Not what seems fair, but what is true;
Not what we dream, but good we do—
These are the things that shine like gems,
Like stars, in Fortune's diadems.

Not as we take, but as we give;
Not as we pray, but as we live—
These are the things that make for peace,
Both now and after Time shall cease.

—CLARENCE URMY

Against a background of false choices—choices that *count* against the soul—Clarence Urmy traces an upward curve in the ascending scale of life's values. His topmost note is reached in the opening couplet of the concluding stanza. "Not as we take, but as we give; not as we pray, but as we live."

What is worth while? This is an age-old question. Whether we be facing the dawn or watching the sunset of human existence, life is still before as. This we know, for each day is itself a little life. It is not the *quantity* but the *quality* of life that counts. If we can *lift the quality ever so little*, its quantity may be disregarded altogether.

Maxims of living have their worth and rules their use. Yet there is a more excellent way. It is the Way of Adventure, the commitment of the soul to the guidance of the Master of the souls of men. This is theme of John Oxenham's searching words:

> To every man there openeth
> A way, and ways, and *a Way*.
> And the high soul climbs the high way,
> And the low soul gropes the low;
> And in between, on the misty flats,
> The rest drift to and fro.
> But to every man there openeth
> A high way and a low,
> And every man decideth
> The way his soul shall go.

As thy days, so shall thy strength be.
—Deuteronomy 33:25

The Burden of the Hour

God broke the years to hours and days,
That hour by hour
And day by day,
Just going on a little way,
We might be able all along
To keep quite strong.
Should all the weights of life
Be laid across our shoulders, and the future, rife
With woe and struggle, meet us face to face
At just one place,
We could not go;
Our feet would stop. And so
God lays a little on us every day,
And never, I believe, on all the way,
Will burdens bear so deep,
Or path-ways lie so steep,
But we can go, if by God's power
We only bear the burden of the hour.

—George Klingle

NOTE ON BURDENS

If we study the problem of burden-bearing, some vital principles emerge.

We find, for example, that it is when we take the burdens of *yesterday* and the burdens of *tomorrow* and pile them on the shoulders of *today*, that we fall beneath their weight.

But even the burdens of today we need not bear alone. How can we lighten them?

Christ bids us share his burden and thus forget our own. What is his burden? Is it not the burden of unselfish love and unremitting service in a world of dark-browed care that knows not yet the secret of his peace?

Surely in his companionship the "yoke is easy and the burden light" for each struggling heart that lifts *with* him the weight and sorrow of the world.

> *Yesterday is already a dream, and*
> *Tomorrow is only a vision;*
> *But today, well lived, makes every*
> *Yesterday a dream of happiness*
> *And every tomorrow a vision of hope*
> *Look well, therefore, to this day.*

They that wait upon the Lord shall renew their strength.
—Isaiah 40:31

Wandering Thoughts

Wandering thoughts are only the echoes of the world made more noticeable by the quiet in which you find yourself. If you do not worry they will die down and a healing stillness will reign in your soul. And as for a temporary inability to pray, it may be met by practicing the art of remaining silent. If you cannot speak to God, it may be God's opportunity to speak to you. Thousands of Christian mystics have loved the words, "Be still, and know that I am God," because they have learned how when a man's eyes are averted from worldly things and directed in silence into his own heart, the presence of God in the soul becomes a realized and experienced fact.

—PETER GREEN

You cannot capture vagrant thoughts by trailing after them. They will only lead you farther and farther afield.

Open the door of the mind to the presence of some great master-thought. Presently its unifying power will be felt. You will no more *be lulled by a dream but led by a vision.*

Surely something like this must be meant by that great word of St. Paul, where be speaks of "bringing every thought into captivity to the obedience of Christ."

> *"Turn your eyes upon Jesus,*
>   *Look full in His wonderful face,*
> *And the things of earth will grow*
>   *strangely dim*
>   *In the light of His glory and grace."*

Jesus Christ. the same yesterday and today and forever.
—Heb. 13:8

Fellowship Evening Hymn

O Jesus, who art ever near
 Though veiled to mortal sight,
Be with us as we gather here
 In evening's fading light.

We kneel, dear Lord, as those of old
 Knelt lowly at Thy side;
The shadows touch earth's gates of gold,
 But Thee they cannot hide.

Refresh our minds and build anew
 These temples of the dust;
Teach us what Thou wouldst have us do
 In lives of simple trust.

Thou art the same, O Christ, today
 As in the distant past;
And Thou hast: said that Thou wilt stay
 With hearts that hold Thee fast!

—J. WILMER GRESHAM

What was the power that renewed the life, sweetened the fellowship, and inspired the adventure of the earliest followers of Jesus?

Was it not an energy that flowed from the conviction that the Master himself was *still* in their midst?

The Fellowship Evening Hymn is built upon this thought. He is here, though veiled to mortal sight. And he is the same, "yesterday and today and forever."

Brother Lawrence wrote "The Practice of the Presence of God." But God *has made himself articulate* in the Incarnation. To Christian experience it is always the practice of the presence of God *in Christ*. Christ is the channel of the life of God. More than that, he is the life itself.

The Sun of righteousness shall arise with healing in its wings.
—Malachi 4:2.

Life's Healing Forces

There is an immense healing power hidden away in every department of the world's life and available for every circumstance of it.

When we have had the body laid low by all manner of ailments and yet have survived; when fate's plow—share has gone clean through one after another of our most cherished projects, leaving us—as we discover afterwards—not one penny the worse; when, after our inmost affections have been smitten by shattering bereavements, we rise from the blow not only still loving, but still enjoying, we become conscious of a *vis medicatrix naturae*, of a vast system and force of healing, spread through the whole constitution of things.

Is there anything in the world so tender, so entirely motherly, as that caress with which nature, when we are sick or overwrought, woos us back to strength?

It is tasted by the man who flies for recovery to his Healer, when on the sea or meeting the keen breeze of the moorland, knows that every breath he draws, every glint of the open heaven, every bit of scenery his eye rests upon, every moment of the delicious resting-time, is forming part of the one great system of beneficence that is working to make him well.

—J. Brierly

The writer—one of the most stimulating of English essayists in the field of religion—asks, "Is there anything in the world so tender, so entirely motherly, as that caress with which Nature, when we are sick or overwrought, woos us back to strength?"

If, as St. John tells us in his doctrine of the Logos—Christ is the instrument of God's creative processes—may we not think of Nature as the *hem of his garment*, or indeed as the *very garment itself*, woven throughout in living beauty, and without seam in the unity of its perfectness?

The woman in the story murmured, "I cannot reach his blessed presence; the crowd is too great; the procession is moving on; I am so crippled by this wretched infirmity. If I can but *touch the hem of his robe* I shall be healed." Nature, in the mystery of its healing life, is the garment of the Great Physician. This sublime thought threads its way through all the sacred literature of the Book of Books. A healing tree sweetened the bitter waters of Marah. The despairing Elijah was sent to Nature, the gentle nurse, who prescribed pure air, wholesome food, untroubled sleep, a long walk over the trail that led to the Mount of God. The Syrian leper was told to dip in the muddy Jordan, the blind man in the pool of Siloam.

Jesus was no stranger to the healing ministries of Nature. The virtue that went forth from his presence and his touch was nurtured and fed in God's temple of the out-of-doors. And so "the healing of his seamless robe is by our beds of pain; we touch him in life's throng and press—and we are whole again."

41

Bless the Lord, O my soul, and forget not all His benefits.
—Psalm 103:2

A Little Te Deum
of the Commonplace

With hearts responsive
And enfranchised eyes,
We thank Thee, Lord, . . .

For all things beautiful, and good, and true,
For things that seemed not good yet turned to
good;
For all the sweet compulsions of Thy will
That chased, and tried, and wrought us to Thy
shape;
For things unnumbered that we take of right,
And value first when first they are withheld;
For light and air; sweet sense of sound and smell;
For ears to hear the heavenly harmonies;
For eyes to see the unseen in the seen;
For vision of The Worker in the work;
For hearts to apprehend Thee everywhere;
We thank Thee, Lord!

—John Oxenham

NOTE ON THANKSGIVING

The psychology of thanksgiving is a most revealing study.

Not only does thanksgiving register our gratitude for benefits received. It touches springs of receptivity in the soul and releases new powers of helpfulness.

John Oxenham, poet-laureate of the world-war, writes of his great happiness in having his "little Te Deum" included in the Wings of Healing.

Traverse the field of thanksgiving with this true poet of the spiritual life. New strength and inspiration will rest upon your heart.

Thanks*giving* will pass into thanks*living*.

Pilate therefore said unto Him, "Art thou a king, then?"
Jesus answered, "Thou sayest that I am a king. To this end
was I born, and for this cause came I into the world, that I
should bear witness unto the truth."—St. John 18:37

The Path of Duty

Not once or twice in our rough island story
The path of Duty was the way to glory.
He that walks it, only thirsting
For the right, and learns to deaden
Love of self, before his journey closes
He shall find the stubborn thistle bursting
Into glossy purples, which outredden
All voluptuous garden roses.
Not once or twice in our fair island-story
The path of Duty was the way to glory.
He, that ever following her commands,
On with toil of heart and knees and hands,
Thro' the long gorge to the far light has won
His path upward, and prevail'd,
Shall find the toppling crags of Duty scaled
Are close upon the shining table-lands
To which our God Himself is moon and sun.

—*TENNYSON*

Tennyson's lines—from the Ode to Duty—on the Death of the Duke of Wellington—recall England's stubborn resistance to her aggressors in these latter days through "blood and toil and sweat and tears." The following highlight in a Christmas broadcast of King George VI would seem to belong to this note.

"I said to the man who stood at the gate of the years: 'Give me light, that I may tread softly into the Unknown,' and he replied, 'Go out into the darkness, and put your hand into the hand of God. That shall be to you better than light and safer than the known way.'"

Wordsworth speaks of duty as the "stern daughter of the voice of God."

The question with many of us is not of *duty* but of *duties*. We find ourselves bewildered by the variety of claims upon our time and interest. Many things must be done imperfectly, or not done at all.

There are two simple rules that lie close at hand.

The first is the rule of "first things first." That is the rule of *priority*. The second is the rule of "doing the next thing." That is the rule of *immediacy*.

> *Do it immediately,*
> *Do it with prayer,*
> *Do it reliantly,*
> *Casting off care;*
> *Do it with reverence,*
> *Tracing His hand*
> *Who hath placed it before thee*
> *With earnest command.*
> *Stayed in omnipotence*
> *Safe 'neath His wing,*
> *Leave all resultings—*
> *Do the next thing.*

A cup of cold water only. —St. Matthew 10-42

The Greatness of
Little Things

In the trivial round and common task of everyday existence there are countless opportunities for becoming Christlike. The look of sympathy, the word of encouragement, the little nameless unremembered acts of love and tenderness, these are the best indications that the vision of Christ has been seen. The great deed, done perhaps in a moment of enthusiasm, is as nothing compared with the patient, thankless endurance of the rubs and worries of a teasing household. Just as the clay and sand, which we so carelessly tread under foot, are the materials that build up the sapphire and the opal, so out of the rags and tatters of daily life we make the moral fibre which we call character. There is no mistake more fatal than to despise the day of small things. Mathematicians speak of infinitesimals, quantities so small as to be insignificant for all practical purposes. But in the mathematics of character there are no infinitesimals. The most trivial act is a step down towards zero. or a step up towards infinity.

—JOHN FEARNLEY

NOTE ON THE GREATNESS OF LITTLE THINGS

Let us not overlook the healing values that lie close to the world of *little things*. If life is fundamental to all health and healing the so-called *trivialities* of daily existence are *points of manifestation* of that life.

The passage an The Greatness of Little Things is taken from *The Road to Damascus*, by John Fearnley. The author writes of the "Vision and the Voice and the Presence" of Christ.

The little book, now out of print, breathes the purity of the "mountain-top" where it was written long, long ago.

The Spirit of "the mountain" *lives* in Gardiner Tucker's well-known lines:

> *"A towered city set within a wood,*
> *Far from the world upon the mountain's crest;*
> *There storms of life burst not, nor cares intrude;*
> *There learning dwells, and peace is wisdom's guest."*

The City of Man

The poets have dreamed of a City of God
    Where the night is as fair as the day;
Where sorrow and sighing have winged their
    swift flight,
    And earth's tears have been all wiped away.

But a City of God in a Kingdom of dreams,
    Like the silvery gleam of a star,
Is far from the City of Man that we know
    In the kingdom of things as they are.

Yet the City of God is not far away,
    Like some dim distant light that we scan;
We are building the City of God every day
    When we serve in the City of Man.

The gold in the streets of the City of Man,
    With its shadowing pain and its needs,
Is the gold of our love for hearts that are
    crushed,
    And the glint of our own golden deeds.

—J. WILMER GRESHAM

The City of Man, and the tender lines of George Stirling that follow here, were written for the Community Chest of San Francisco.

Here is a question which is often asked in the recurring appeals that come for the support of social welfare agencies. How *can giving through organized channels of relief* be made as personal as if our own outstretched hand touched the objects of our compassion?

The answer is, only by conceiving the poor, the maimed, the sick, the unfortunate, as our *very own*, as near and dear as the *blood ties* that bind us to mother, sister, father, brother. This was the teaching of the Master.

Were it your mother on the bed of pain,
Were it your sister on the wolfish street,
We would not wait your charity in vain:
To give were more than sweet.

Were it your father broken by the task,
Were it your brother ailing and adrift,
How brief a moment should we need to ask
The sympathetic gift!

And these, for whom we beg compassion here,
In them an equal power of suffering lies,
And hearts now helpless dust have held them dear.
Can we do otherwise?

He shall cover thee with His feathers, and under
His wings shalt thou trust. —Psalm 91:4

The Eternal Goodness

I know not where His islands lift
  Their fronded palms in air;
I only know I cannot drift
  Beyond His love and care.

O brothers! If my faith is vain,
  If hopes like these betray,
Pray for me that my feet may gain
  The sure and safer way.

And thou, O Lord! by whom are seen
  Thy creatures as they be,
Forgive me if too close I lean
  My human heart on Thee.

—JOHN GREENLEAF WHITTIER

St. Paul writes that we should "comfort others with the comfort wherewith we ourselves have been comforted of God."

This is the secret of the healing comfort that runs like a thread of gold through all the poetry of Whittier.

We can impart only that which has been communicated to us, whether of knowledge, of vision, or of sympathy.

The lines, "I know not where His islands lift their fronded palms in air—I only know I cannot drift beyond His love and care," have brought solace to nameless thousands of God's children.

COMFORT AND PEACE
from God

Come ye yourselves apart . . . and rest awhile
—St. Mark 6:31

What is Lent?

*L*ent is a season of spiritual adventure. The Master in the wilderness forgot even about the staff of physical life—*bread*, by which man surely lives. *Why?* Because he was keen about the quest—the adventure—for God. So, then, we enter the Lenten season not to discipline ourselves by fasting, and not to make ourselves like him by imitating his discipline, *but to make* our great adventure *into the depths of God's being and our own,* and incidentally, *only incidentally,* do we find ourselves *giving up this thing and letting go that*— our time, our selfish vanities, our very food itself. Why? *All because we are keen about the quest,* the quest for God. In the light of this affirmation the season of Lent loses the painful artificiality with which it is so often invested.

—J. WILMER GRESHAM

NOTE ON LENT

The paragraph about Lent is inserted to stress a principle rather than to mark a season. This is not to belittle the season, but to claim its larger meaning, and to relate it to all our Christian living.

Whenever we bend our energies upon something supremely worthwhile we automatically let many other things go. That is the Lenten principle. If this be true, there is a place—a quiet, secret place—for Lent throughout the year, with all its weeks and days.

Sacrifice for discipline has its values. But sacrifice as incidental to the pursuit of noble purposes is priceless. Indeed, we think not of it as sacrifice. If we think of it at all, it is as a bit of a gift that goes with the offering of ourselves.

Lord, teach us to pray. —*St. Luke 11: 1*

The Adventure of Prayer
(Part One)

Prayer is being with God.

You can't choose at all about it, except just in choosing to be with him.

Perhaps he will take you up on the mountain with him.

Perhaps he will take you into the night with him, or into the mist where you will not be able to see him.

Perhaps you will be with him in pain, or in exaltation, or in happiness, or in tiredness.

He just says: "Come to me," and you say: "I will," or "I will not."

You make no stipulations, that is not your part; you know that he wants you, and you know what kind of wanting that is.

You know that if you say you will not come he does not leave off wanting you, so you imagine what that means.

Prayer finds its highest meaning as an act of communion with God.

Christ's prayer of intercession in the 17th chapter of St. John illustrates this. But that communion did not stand alone.

Those sacred hours of fellowship led to the world's greatest act of service. The prayer was uttered as the night of Gethsemane passed into the day of the supreme sacrifice.

An adventure of prayer is an adventure of faith, and a wise teacher in the field of Christian thought has significantly said:

"It is by no means enough to set out cheerfully with your God on an adventure of faith. Nothing will fall out as you expect. Your Guide will keep to no beaten path. He will lead you by a way such as you never dreamed your eyes would look upon.

"He knows no fear and he expects you to fear nothing while he is with you. The clinging hand of his child makes a desperate situation a delight to him. It is your business to learn to be peaceful and safe in God in every situation ... Whatever his questions or his reticences we may be absolutely sure of an unperplexed and undismayed Saviour."

The Adventure of Prayer
(Part Two)

You know that if you come to him he will ask you to help him about the Kingdom, that he will in the end give you that work for it that no one else can do.

You know that he will bring you into the Fellowship of his friends, and that you will be allowed to bring him into the Fellowship of your friends.

But, of course, you will also go with him before his enemies; and the things that they say about him will be said about you.

And you will also go among the people who don't care, whom he is trying to arouse to a sense of his Love.

Quite often he and you will be left desolate with the doors locked before you, and the people on the other side scornful and amused.

"Greater love hath no man than this, that a man lay down his life for his friends.

"Ye are my friends, if ye do whatsoever I command you.

"Henceforth I call you friends, for all things that I have heard of my Father I have made known unto you"

These parting words of the Master tell us that in the training of his followers friendship was the topmost level of their relation to him.

To be a disciple was a privilege. To be an apostle was a distinction. But to be his *friend* was the richest gift of all.

It is easy to sing "What a Friend we have in Jesus!" The question is, *what sort of friends has he in us?*

The Adventure of Prayer
(Part Three)

You will find that he will ask you to do things which you can only do if you forget about yourself and the sort of person you thought you were, or he may ask you to face death or complete shame as he does himself.

And all the time you will fail him so often that by and by you will have no self-confidence left, only a growing confidence in him instead, because *he* does not fail *you*.

And prayer must be fearfully difficult, because it isn't easy to be with God, although it is simple.

It means that some things must go, like pride, unkindness, and self-indulgence, and self-importance.

But all the same it is a choice which the best part of you wants, so that the most glorious souls in all the ages do choose the Adventure of Prayer.

—Margaret Cropper

Entering the circle of his friends means taking to heart the welfare of his Kingdom.

The time is short, and there is much to be done. No friend of his can *acquiesce in things as they are*. Loyalty to the King means a willingness to class as "lesser loyalties" a world of interests that must henceforth take second place.

This will not be hard to do; for if they are true and right the larger loyalty will hold them in its clasp. These lesser loyalties are kingdoms to be won for him.

Thou wilt keep him in perfect peace, whose mind is
stayed on Thee. —Isaiah 26:3

God Understands

It is so sweet to know,
When we are tired, and when the hand of pain
Lies on our hearts, and when we look in vain
For human comfort, that the Heart Divine
Still understands these cares of yours and mine.

Not only understands, but day by day
Lives with us while we tread the earthly way,
Bears with us all our weariness and feels
The shadow of the faintest cloud that steals
Across our sunshine; ever learns again
The depth and bitterness of human pain.

—*ANON.*

NOTE ON GOD'S UNDERSTANDING

That God *knows* and that he *cares* are two fixed points in the approach of the soul to him.

"The Father knoweth that ye have need of all these things." These were the words of the Master touching the outer fringe of our material wants. But the teaching of the Master went further. He spoke of the Father's provision for *spiritual things* as well. This was the message of that octave of blessedness that we call the Beatitudes.

Further still, Christ's revelation of the Father portrayed the solicitude of an understanding Heart—his "feeling for our weariness and the faintest shadow that steals across the sunshine of our lives—and all the depth and bitterness of our human pain."

In the Stillness

Lord, in the stillness of this holy place,
Borne up on wings of prayer,
Gone like a shadow is each lingering trace
Of doubt and grief and care.

Now in the hush of falling eventide,
When fevered pulses cease,
O let my spirit in Thy keeping hide,
Strong in Thy changeless peace.

And when the toilsome day hath run its race,
Lost in the silent night,
Keep Thou the radiant vision of Thy face
Undimmed before my sight.

At Holy Communion:

Here in remembrance is Thy Table spread,
And by Thine own dear sign
Lord, Thou art present in the broken Bread
And in the poured out Wine.

—*J. Wilmer Gresham*

Withdraw to some silent place, where you can be utterly alone, free from all mental or physical disturbance.

Gradually surrender your mind into a state of absolute quiet. Allow your entire being to be enveloped in the atmosphere of the love of God.

Actively seek to sense the presence of the Father. You will discover the hidden meaning of life. You will achieve a better understanding of the work that lies before you in the world. You will hear the Voice of God.

> *"And so I come for deeper rest to this still room;*
> *For, here, the habit of the soul*
> *Feels less the outer world's control,*
> *And from the silence, multiplied*
> *By these still forms on every side,*
> *The world that time and sense have known*
> *Falls off and leaves us, God, alone."*

The Music in a Rest

There is no music in a *rest*, but there is the making of music in it. In our whole life-melody the music is broken off here and there by *rests* and we foolishly think we have come to the end of the theme. God sends a time of forced leisure, sickness, disappointed plans, frustrated efforts, and makes a sudden pause in the choral hymn of our lives; and we lament that our voices must be silent, and our part missing in the music which ever goes up to the ear of the Creator. How does the musician read the *rest*? See him beat the time with unvarying count, and catch up the next note true and steady, as if no breaking place had come between.

Not without design does God write the music of our lives. Be it ours to learn the tune, and not be dismayed at the *rests*. They are not to be slurred over, not to be omitted, not to destroy the melody, not to change the keynote. If we look up, God himself will beat the time for us. With the eye on him, we shall strike the next note full and clear. If we sadly say to ourselves, *there is no music in a rest*, let us not forget *there is the making of music in it*. The making of music is often a slow and painful process in this life. How patiently God works to teach us. How long he waits for us to learn the lesson.

—*JOHN RUSKIN*

NOTE ON THE MUSIC IN A REST

It has been said that the universe is woven throughout by a single hand. Nowhere is this more apparent than in the fact that when we examine its texture we find each seemingly separate thing *related* to something else. 'We might call this the principle of *relatedness*—not relativity. Only a few highly scientific minds can explain the theory of relativity as it effects the movements of the heavenly bodies. And we can safely leave it to the mathematics of the astronomer—and be guided by his conclusions. But the fact that each thing is *related to something else* is a matter of common observation and experience.

When Ruskin tells us that there is no music in a *rest*—but the *making of music* in it—his meaning is quite clear. He means that a rest in music is related to the notes that lead to it and that follow it. In other words, it does not exist *for itself.*

Upon the simplicity of this truth the author of *Ethics of the Dust* builds a parable of life. If God made provision for rest—and *only* rest—existence would be stagnation. Rest is related to action, just as sleep to waking, and even the incident of death to immortality.

We cannot say too much for silence-and entering into the silence. Someone reminds us that silence is "like the sleeping seas. It gathers to itself calmness and strength. It rests upon peace and beauty. It is the whisper of endless time. It is the purifier of men's souls. It is the mighty force that bears human souls to the realms of greatness." Not only should we enter into the silence. The silence should enter into us.

"If chosen men had never been alone,
In deep mid-silence opendoored to God,
No greatness ever had been dreamed or done."

All of which is divinely true. But the greatness that is born of silence is not for itself. It is related to achievement. It is but a pause—whether momentary or prolonged—and it stands in measured relation to the music in which it is set.

Let the peace of God rule in your hearts.
—Colossians 3:15

Peace and Joy

Peace does not mean the end of all our striving;
Joy does not mean the drying of our tears,
Peace is the power that comes to souls arriving
Up to the light where God Himself appears.
Joy is the wine that God is ever pouring
Into the hearts of those that strive with Him,
Opening their eyes to vision and adoring,
Strengthening their arms to warfare glad and grim.
Bread of Thy Body give me for my fighting,
Give me to drink Thy sacred Blood for wine;
While there are wrongs that need me for the
righting,
While there is warfare splendid and divine.
Give me for light the sunshine of Thy sorrow,
Give me for shelter the shadow of Thy Cross,
Give me to share the glory of tomorrow,
And gone from my heart is the bitterness of loss.

—G. A. Studdert Kennedy

NOTE ON PEACE

Shortly before his lamented death, the late G. A. Studdert-Kennedy wrote of his pleasure in having the lines on the preceding page included in the Wings of Healing.

When we study the spirit of the poem we are reminded of what the mystics say of the *central peace of God*. They assure us that the central peace of God is not the peace that follows pain; nor the peace that succeeds some crisis of life; nor the peace that comes after some danger has disappeared.

The central peace of God descends upon the soul in the *midst* of all these things. That is why it is called the peace that passeth all understanding.

The other forms of peace the world can sometimes give—and often take away.

But this is the peace of Christ, who says "not as the world giveth give I unto you."

"If peace be in the heart,
The wildest storm is full of solemn beauty,
The midnight flash but shows the path of duty,
Each living creature tells some new and joyous story,
The very trees and stones all catch a ray of glory,
It peace be in the heart."

Pray one for another, that ye may be healed. —St. James 5:16.

The Meaning of Intercession

Intercessory prayer is not a scattering of good wishes in the air toward some one we desire to serve. Neither is it the vocal or silent utterance of pious hopes in the direction of God.

It is the orderly operation of a vital energy, an immediate transmitting of life, where the person prayed for is actively receptive, and the creation of fresh opportunity for him, whatever his temper of mind.

By the force of spiritual projection, which eliminates space by ignoring it, I lay my life over against that of my friend, simultaneously establishing definite and conscious contact with God. Intercessory prayer makes personality a sacrament. Our life becomes open for God's use in the bestowal of his gifts. We become agents of power for others. Thus prayer takes on a new and inspiring meaning. God's strength, God's love, God's healing life, flow through us to others.

—CHARLES H. BRENT

NOTE ON THE MEANING OF INTERCESSION

Prayer has many aspects-many angles. *When we enter the school of prayer*, with the Master of life as our teacher, we are at the beginning of a long, long process of tuition. We look up into the Master's face with the simplicity and directness of a child. Our thought is just to listen to him—or to talk to him or be silent in his wondrous presence.

But we must not forget that we have entered the *school of prayer*. For soon we find ourselves moving upward from the *child-garden* to the *primary*, and then to *higher grades in Christ's prayer-school of the soul*.

Presently we learn the *fellowship of prayer* as we look around us in the schoolroom—or beyond the schoolroom to those who strive or suffer in the world.

But not until the Master shows us how *intercession* is woven into the pattern of the prayer-life is commencement-day in sight. Then what the Father hath revealed to the Master is made known to us. The crowning lesson that we learn is that *in intercession we become the medium through which God sends his quickening impulses to those for whom we pray*.

Thus we no longer ask his gifts for ourselves, but for others. We *visualize others and their needs*, one by one. Thus visualizing them, the last vestige of our own besetting needs is effaced, and a strange, mystic, wondrous thing takes place. Being the instruments of God's life-communication to others, we ourselves—quite unconsciously—are changed into the image of the divine Intercessor, the Master in the school of prayer. We learn the highest meaning of sharing, the sharing of his ministry of healing and of help.

Of Deepest Worth

These are the things I prize
    And hold of deepest worth:
Light of the sapphire skies,
    Peace of the silent hills,
Shelter of forest, comfort of the grass,
Shadow of clouds that swiftly pass,
    And after showers
    The smell of flowers,
        And of the good brown earth
    And best of all, along the way,
        Friendship and mirth.

—HENRY VAN DYKE

NOTE ON THE THINGS I PRIZE

In a letter to the Wings of Healing, Dr. Henry van Dyke reminds us that the lines beginning "These are the Things I Prize" should he quoted as part of the ode, "God of the Open Air."

The entire poem should be read for its healing spirit and its power "to knit up the ravelled sleeve of care."

Close your eyes in the stillness of some quiet time or place. Slowly recall the poet's lines. The peace of the silent hills will steal over you. Under the "shelter of forest and shadow of clouds you will find yourself in communion with the "God of the Open Air."

Out of the hush of that communion will come "friendship and mirth" and the companionship of the Master of men.

My presence shall go with thee, and I will give thee rest. —Exodus 33:14

Miracles

Thy miracles in Galilee
When all the world went after Thee
To bless their sick, to touch their blind,
O Gracious Healer of Mankind
But fan my faith to brighter glow!
Have I not seen, do I not know
One greater miracle than these?
That Thou, the Lord of Life, shouldst please
To walk beside me all the way,
My Comrade of the Everyday!

Was I not blind to beauty too
Until Thy love came shining through
The dark of self and made me see
I share a glorious world with Thee?
Did I not falter till Thy hand
Reached out to mine? Did I not stand
Perplexed and mute and deaf until
I heard Thy gentle "Peace, be still,"
And all the turmoil of my heart
Was silenced and I found my part?

Those other miracles I know
Were far away, were long ago,
But this, that I may see Thy face
Transforming all the commonplace,
May work with Thee, and watch Thee bless
My little loaves in tenderness;
This sends me singing on my way,
O Comrade of the Everyday!

—MOLLY ANDERSON HALEY

This tender poem interprets with singular felicity the spirit of the Ministry of Healing.

In her "Garden Hymn" and in 'The Architect," which complete her offering to the Wings of Healing, there are other phases of Mrs. Haley's message.

"The Miracles" is a transcript *from experience* in lines of exquisite verse.

To know the Master as "The Comrade of the Everyday" is to see things with his eyes and to share his work of "transforming all the commonplace."

For those who weak and broken lie,
In weariness and agony
Great Healer, to their beds of pain
Come, touch, and make them whole again.
O hear a people's prayers, and bless
Thy servants in their hour of stress!

Blessed are the pure in heart for they shall see God.
—St. Matthew 5:8

Breathe on us,
Breath of God

Breathe on us, breath of God,
    Till we are wholly Thine.
Till all this earthly part of us
    Glows with Thy fire divine!

Breathe on us, breath of God!
    Fill us with life anew;
That we may love what Thou dost love,
    And do what Thou wouldst do.

Breathe on us, breath of God,
    Until our hearts are pure;
Until with Thee we will one will
    To do and to endure.

Breathe on us, breath of God—
    So shall we never die;
But live with Thee the perfect life
    Of Thine eternity.

—EDWIN HATCH

The hymn, "Breathe on us, breath of God," is an invocation to the Holy Spirit.

Always, with the restoration of the ministry of healing, there comes a recognition of the place and power of the Holy Spirit.

And always, the action of the Spirit is likened to the breathing of God's life-giving breath. It is the quickening Spirit, underneath all of the functions and processes of our manifold being, that makes possible the healing of body and soul.

The physical agencies of healing in medicine and surgery, and in all the fields of therapeutic science, find their value and their place in *rectifying channels* for the liberation of the healing stream of life. But *it is life itself which heals.*

An Evening Prayer

If I have wounded any soul today,
If I have caused one foot to go astray,
If I have walked in my own wilful way—
    Good Lord forgive!

If I have uttered idle words or vain,
If I have turned aside from want or pain
Lest I myself should suffer through the strain—
    Good Lord forgive!

If I have craved for joys that are not mine,
If I have let my wayward heart repine,
Dwelling on things on earth, not things divine—
    Good Lord forgive!

Forgive the sins I have confessed to Thee
Forgive the secret sins I do not see;
For which I know not, Father, teach Thou me—
    Help me to live.

—*C. Maude Battersby*

The Evening Prayer on the preceding page is a prayer for forgiveness at the close of day.

There is a vital connection between forgiveness and healing. One follows the other by a natural sequence. "Bless the Lord, O my soul," said the Psalmist, "who *forgiveth* all thy sin and *healeth* all thine infirmities." God *first* forgives and *then* heals.

And the quiet evening-time, with its backward look over the record of the day, summons us to thoughtful sorrow for opportunities neglected, or time misspent, or grief or hurt that has come to the world through us.

Then comes the night. But the night that falls upon a forgiven spirit will wrap the soul in peace. Healing will follow in the footsteps of pardon. And presently a bright new day will summon to a nobler task.

We know that, when He shall appear, we shall be like Him;
for we shall see Him as He is. —I John 3-2

The Vision

Two friends in Athens were once discussing the ennobling influence of Greek art. In the course of the conversation one of them said:

"I came here on a hiking tour with a chap who was not making as much of himself as he should have done. But he went away a changed man, mentally and morally strong, physically perfect. You would never guess what it was that did it."

"He saw a statue of one of the Greek gods in the museum. Studying it closely, he found that it showed certain muscles that he could not find in his own body.

"He told me that he was going to train down till those muscles did show. He stopped drinking and loafing to do it. He took to exercising and walking, and rowing and swimming and boxing.

"By the time the muscles showed out clear and strong he was so keen over life that he wanted to make the most out of it. And, as I have said, he has done it.

"The vision of physical perfection changed that man's life. He saw what he was, and what he wanted to be. And be went to work and made himself as the statue of that Greek god, with all the hidden strength that it expressed."

Christ holds before us his wondrous human life, his perfect manhood in all of the strength of its purity and loveliness. And he says, "This is what you ought to be. This is what you can be. This is your true life."

This reading in the "Wings" relates the story of a statue of a Greek god that touched a young man's imagination and changed his life. What has that to do with the vision of the Healing Christ to which this little book is dedicated? To answer this, we must note the distinction between imagination and vision.

Among other things, imagination may he said to be that mysterious faculty within us by which we project upon the screen of our conscious thought the *image* of what lies in the path of possible achievement. And what imagination is to the mind, *vision* is to the soul.

When the soul of man catches the vision of the Image of Christ—and adores it—a subtle spiritual process begins, a process of transformation. "Reflecting as in a mirror the glory of Christ we are changed into the same image from character to character." Note, *we are changed*—we do not change ourselves.

The statue of the Greek god wrought upon the imagination of the young man and slowly changed his body into the glory of what he saw. The Vision Beautiful of the perfection of Christ likewise beckons the soul. The cleansing and healing properties then enact their soul-transforming work until the body itself becomes a living temple, strong and divinely beautiful.

God's Signal in Prayer

I cannot tell why there should come to me
    A thought of some one miles and miles away,
In swift insistence on the memory,
    Unless a need there be that I should pray.

Too hurried oft are we to spare the thought,
    For days together, of some friend away;
Perhaps God does it for us, and we ought
    To read His signal as a call to pray.

Perhaps, just then, a friend has fiercer fight,
    And more appalling weakness, and decay
Of courage, darkness, some lost sense of right,
    And so, because he needs my prayer, I pray.

Friend, do the same for me. If I intrude
    Unasked upon you, on some crowded day,
Give me a moment's prayer as interlude;
    Be very sure I need it, therefore pray.

Prayer signals are calls to intercession. Oftentimes they fail to reach us. We are too dull—or we fail to listen. We pass them by; or *they pass us by*, finding reception elsewhere.

Our failure to heed prayer-signals is a serious loss to ourselves as well as to those for whom we ought to pray.

Intercession is like a triangle. The three points are God, friend, and self. Of course God can reach our friends directly, without our intervention. But in that case the triangle is broken. Prayer becomes only a vertical line of individual approach. *Fellowship and intercession* are lost.

Let us learn to *read the signals*.

The Lord thy God will hold thy right hand, saying unto thee,
Fear not; I will help thee. —Isaiah 41:13

Guidance

Father, hold Thou my hands. The way is steep,
I cannot see the path my feet must keep!
I cannot tell, so dark the tangled way,
Where next to step. Oh, stay,
Come close; take both my hands in Thine,
          Make Thy way mine!

Lead me! I may not stay—
I must move on. But, oh, the way!
I must be brave and go;
Step forward in the dark, nor know
If I shall reach the goal at all—
If I shall fall!

Take Thou my hand—
Take it; Thou knowest best
How I shall go, and all the rest.
I cannot, cannot see!
Lead on! I hold my hands to Thee—
I own no will but Thine!

"Make Thy Way Mine,"—KLINGLE

The soliloquy on the opposite page is in the spirit of the Master's prayer in the garden.

In the garden the Master's closest friends could go with him only a certain distance. He must be alone with God. They must not *hear*, though they might *overhear* what he said in prayer.

So with ourselves. Deep as the sorrow of the world may rest upon our hearts, there are times when our personal relation to his purposes demands that we be alone with him.

It is then that we say: "Father, hold Thou my hands—and feet—my life itself."

The Adventure

I love to think of them at dawn
Beneath the frail pink sky,
Casting their nets in Galilee
And fish-hawks circling by.

Casting their nets in Galilee,
Just off the hills of brown;
Such happy, simple fisherfolk,
Before the Lord walked down.

Contented, peaceful fishermen,
Before they ever knew
The peace of God that filled their hearts
Brim-full, and broke them, too.

Young John, who trimmed the flapping sail,
Homeless, in Patmos died.
Peter, who hauled the teeming net,
Head-down, was crucified.

The peace of God, it is no peace,
But strife closed in the sod.
Yet, brothers, pray for but one thing,
The marvelous peace of God.

—W. A. PERCY

They were nearly all in their radiant twenties, those men of Galilee, the earliest followers of the Master.

John who trimmed the flapping sail, Peter who hauled the teeming net—and the others.

They made the great adventure, not for the kingdom, which they never understood, but for the King, to whom they gave their deathless love.

The same call to high adventure rings down the centuries:

"Follow the Christ, the King!
Live pure, speak true, right wrong, follow the
King—else, wherefore born?"

There is a spirit in man; and the inspiration of the Almighty giveth them understanding. —*Job 32:8*

The Spiritual Faculty

When we look closely at Elihu's searching words, we are struck with what we may call their clear and scientific accuracy. "There is a spirit in man"; that is, *there is a spiritual faculty, or faculty for God, in man.* "The inspiration of the Almighty giveth them understanding"; that is, *God purposes to meet the need that he has implanted.* Indeed, is it not a commonplace that, wherever faculties and capacities have been bestowed we may reasonably look for corresponding fields for their employment? Forms of beauty exist for the soul, companionships for the heart, truth for the mind, sound for the ear, light for the eye, and for man's spiritual faculty, or faculty for God, God himself.

But note: the spiritual faculty, like the physical, the mental, the aesthetic, and all the others, may be developed and cultivated, or neglected and lost.

—J. WILMER GRESHAM

Charles Darwin in one of his letters tells us out of his own experience how faculties may be lost through disuse.

He says that "Shakespeare, whom he once took great delight in, eventually became so intolerably dull to him that even the finest of the plays positively distressed him." Besides, he lost his taste for music and art, as well as for poetry. He says that "his mind became a kind of machine for grinding out general laws from large collections of facts;" and that "this seemed to have atrophied that part of the brain upon which the higher tastes depend."

And then he tells us "that if he had to live his life again he would make it a rule to read some poetry and to listen to some music at least once a week so that the parts of the brain now atrophied would thus become active through use."

"The loss of these tastes," he says, "became a loss to happiness, injurious to the intellect, and possibly to the moral nature, because it enfeebled the emotional part of that nature."

May not the spiritual faculty, the faculty for God, follow the same general law?

Live Day by Day

I heard a voice at evening softly say,
   "Bear not thy yesterday into tomorrow;
   Nor load this week with last week's load of
      sorrow.
   Lift all thy burdens as they come, nor try
   To weigh the present with the by and by.
One step and then another, take thy way—
      Live day by day."

    "Live day by day.
Though autumn leaves are withering round
   thy way,
   Walk in the sunshine. It is all for thee.
   Push straight ahead, as long as thou canst see.
   Dread not the winter whither thou mayst go,
   But, when it comes, be thankful for the snow.
Onward and upward. Look and smile
      and pray—
      Live day by day."

—*JULIA HARRIS MAY*

Much has been written upon the thought that "each day is a little life" and that we may safely let the morrow "be anxious for the things of itself."

"One day at a time !
   Whatever its load, whatever its length,
   According to each shall be blessing and strength.

           One day at a time!
           'Tis a wholesome rhyme!
           A good one to live by
           One day at a time!"

There is an inscription on a sundial at the University of Virginia, at Charlottesville, which reads as follows and in this form:

           Time
             is
   Too slow for those who wait,
   Too swift for those who fear,
   Too long for those who grieve,
   Too short for those who rejoice,
   But for those who love, time is
             Eternity.
             Hours fly,
             Flowers die,
             New days,
             New ways,
             Pass by.
             Love stays.

The earth is full of Thy riches. —Psalm 104:24

A Garden Hymn

I never knew Thee, Lord, until
    My garden brought us face to face,
Revealed Thy gracious miracle
    Of sun and seed in little space.

Since I have seen Thine alchemy
    Change earth-blown bulbs to living gold
Of daffodils, Eternity
    Has seemed a simple truth to hold.

The incense-breath of mignonette
    Has summoned me to vespers too.
And may I nevermore forget
    To lift my heart, as pansies do!

No dim cathedral is as still
    As twilight in this holy place;
I never knew Thee, Lord, until
    My garden brought us face to face.

—MOLLY ANDERSON HALEY

Molly Anderson Haley has not only placed three of her lovely poems on the altar of the Wings of Healing, but has written deep and sincere words of appreciation of the book itself.

It is not strange that one should meet the Master in a garden. When we read of the garden of Gethsemane, we think of a garden of sorrow.

But we read that Jesus *ofttimes frequented* that garden. There were times before the night of his passion "when no dim cathedral was as still as twilight in that holy place," and the garden brought him "face to face with God." Did not Mary mistake him for the *gardener* on the resurrection morning?

If the "leaves of the tree of life are for the healing of the nations," what shall we say of the ministry of form and color and fragrance when a garden's beauty brings us face to face with God?

"The kiss of the sun for pardon,
The song of the bird for mirth,
You are nearer God's heart in a garden,
Than anywhere else on earth."

COURAGE
for Our Daily Walk

A merry heart maketh a cheerful countenance.
—Proverbs 15:13

Little Things

A little work, a little play
To keep us going—and so, good-day!

A little warmth, a little light
Of love's bestowing—and so, good-night!

A little fun to match the sorrow
Of each days growing—and so, good-morrow!

A little trust that when we die
We reap our sowing! And so—good-bye!

—GEORGE DU MAURIER

Some of the simplest poems are the tenderest. They are like flowers that might be passed by but for their arresting fragrance.

How easy to learn "by heart" the four brief couplets of Du Maurier, and what a prescription for living they contain!

After all, life is but the *sum of little things*.

There is no great or small to the God that loveth all.

A traveler in the Orient wrote about the poem of the temple-bell. The entire poem consists of a single line: *"The temple bell sounds the loneliness of a thousand years."*

Reading that *one line* you look through its simplicity into its hidden depths.

"You see the crumbling temple in its ancient grove outside the village; the white-robed priest, climbing the flagstones; the wooden clapper, calling out the deep-toned notes of the bronze bell.

"You see forty generations of the dead who heard the same bell, now all gone to their rest; the slow growth of the ancient trees, planted by forgotten men of a forgotten age—*the loneliness of a thousand years.*"

Disposition and Duty

I said "Let me walk in the fields;"
He said, "No, walk in the town;"
I said, "There are no flowers there;"
He said, "No flowers, but a crown."

I said. "But the sky is black—
There is nothing but noise and din;"
He wept as He sent me back;—
"There is more," said He; "there is sin."

I said, "But the air is thick,
And fogs are veiling the sun."
He answered, "Yet hearts are sick,
And souls in the dark undone."

I said, "I shall miss the light,
And friends will miss me, they say;"
He answered, "Choose tonight,
If I am to miss you or they."

I pleaded for time to be given.
He said, "Is it hard to decide?
It will not seem hard in Heaven
To have followed the steps of your Guide."

I cast one look at the fields,
Then set my face to the town;
He said, "My child, do you yield?
Will you leave the flowers for the crown?"

Then into His hand went mine;
And into my heart came He;
And I walk in a light divine,
The path I had feared to see.

—*George MacDonald*

NOTE ON DISPOSITION AND DUTY

It is not for us to decide where we shall walk. whether in green fields or city streets. This is decreed for most of us by circumstance.

George MacDonald's lines have to do with something within ourselves—the old, old question of *disposition and duty*.

The poem is a parable in verse, *disposition* looking toward the sunny countryside, *duty* pointing to the fog-veiled, clamorous marts of men.

The inward problem is an ever-recurring one.

Two elements are involved in a decision—*the will to human service* and the *companionship of the Master*.

Thou wilt keep him in perfect peace whose mind
is stayed on Thee. —Isaiah 26:3

Rest Where You Are

When spurred by tasks unceasing or undone,
You would seek rest afar,
And cannot, 'tho repose be rightly won,
Rest where you are.

Neglect the needless; hallow what remains.
Move without stress or jar
With quiet of a spirit self-possessed,
Rest where you are.

Not in event, restriction, or release,
Not in scenes near or far,
But in yourself is restlessness or peace,
Rest where you are.

Where lives the soul, lives God. His day, His
world
No circumstance need mar.
His starry nights are tents of peace unfurled;
Rest where you are.

—CHARLES POOLE CLEAVES

Rest, we are told, is not inactivity, but the exercise of powers in perfect equilibrium. But this is divine rest, the uncreated rest of God. And it is ours only as we become Godlike.

Humanly there must be fixed times of inactivity, when by a mental act we bring all the motion of the inward life to a quiet pause.

The *inward chamber of rest is unlocked by the key of relaxation.* When its door is open, its stillness pervades the whole house of personality. We *rest where we are.* We need not move into another house in the next street, nor seek lodging in some distant place,

Except the Lord build the house they labor but in vain that build it. —Psalm 127:1

The Architect Divine

I would not call Him in, my heart decried
The use of any plans except my own;
By them I reared and ceiled four walls of stone.
As blindly too I shut myself inside.
No door was there, no casement opening wide
On darkness such as I had never known;
Imprisoned and discouraged and alone
I knelt amid the ruins of my pride.
And then He came, the Architect Divine,
In tenderness surpassing all my dreams.
"I am the Light," He said, "I am the door!"
On that I built anew this house of mine;
My walk became His windows, through them
    streams
The sunlight of His presence more and more.

—MOLLY ANDERSON HALEY

102

Already in the "Wings" you have read the note on Molly Anderson Haley's "Garden Hymn."

In her letter to the "Wings," Mrs. Haley adds a word about "The Architect" which we feel sure she would permit us to publish, and which our readers would not wish to have omitted.

The sonnet was written under the inspiration of a sermon preached by Bishop Stires at the author's confirmation. We offer it to our readers as a theme for meditation.

We, too, have often "built our walls of stone," and "imprisoned and discouraged have knelt amid the ruins of our pride."

"And then He came, the Architect Divine," and our walls "became His windows" with the sunlight of his presence streaming through.

Lo, he enters the earthly house which selfish hands have built for self alone, and it becomes a temple, radiant with the beauty of the King!

Be of good courage and He shall strengthen thine heart.
—Psalm 27:14.

Courage to Live

To those who have tried and seemingly have failed,
Reach out, dear Lord, and comfort them today;
For those whose hope has dimmed, whose faith
    has paled,
Lift up some lighted heavenly torch, I pray.
They are so frightened, Lord; reach out a hand.
They are so hurt and helpless; be their friend.
Baflled and blind, they do not understand;—
They think this dark and tangled road the end.

Oh, touch to flame their hope that has burned
    low,
And strike with fire faith's ashes that are dead.
Let them walk proudly once again, and go
Seeking the sure and steadfast light ahead.
Help them to move among their fellow men
With courage to live, courage to try again.

—GRACE NOLL CROWELL

We have here, in the form of a simple sonnet, a prayer for courage to live. When we look deep into the heart of it, we find that it differs in an important element from many other prayers—and indeed hymns that are known to us.

The title—Courage to Live—is arresting. It strikes a responsive chord within us, and this chord moves through the sonnet to the very last line. It expresses our own need for courage as we face life either in the crisis or the commonplace of each day's challenge to live.

But note—if you will, that this poem-prayer is clearly not a petition for ourselves. Indeed, self does not consciously enter into it. It is an ascending intercession *for others whose courage has failed.* The still, sweet music of humanity pulses in its lines. It speaks for all whose hope has dimmed, whose faith has paled; who are hurt and helpless, baffled, and blind; who think this dark and tangled road the end. We see as in a vision the mutely suffering ones whose hearts are laid bare upon the anvil of circumstance, beaten and bruised, yearning to know the meaning of it all.

We lift them up to God upon the wings of an understanding love. We ask that they may walk proudly once again, that they may move among their fellow-men with courage to live, courage to try again.

Speak, Lord, for Thy servant heareth. —*1 Samuel 3:9*

Walking with God

At cool of day, with God I walk
    My garden's grateful shade;
I hear His voice among the trees,
    And I am not afraid.

He speaks to me in every wind,
    He smiles from every star;
He is not deaf to me, nor blind,
    Nor absent, nor afar.

His hand, that shuts the flowers to sleep,
    Each in its dewy fold,
Is strong my feeble life to keep,
    And competent to hold.

The powers below and powers above,
    Are subject to His care—
I cannot wander from His love
    Who loves me everywhere.

—*MASON*

In the old creation story we read that "God walked in the garden in the cool of day."

Mason's little poem is built upon this thought.

Walking with God is not as easy as it seems. "Can two walk together unless they be agreed?" This was the question that Amos put. There is deep wisdom in it.

Companionship implies mutuality of interest. The companionship of God is a call to the uplands and the heights of thought and feeling. But more than that, it leads to fields of service. After the walk, and after the talk, come the vision and the task.

Better be excused from a closer walk with God than to shun the consequences.

Fight the good fight of faith, lay hold on
eternal life. —1 Timothy 6:12

The Challenge

Be strong!

We are not here to play, to dream, to drift;
We have hard work to do, and loads to lift.
Shun not the struggle, face it, 'tis God's gift.

Be strong!

Say not the days are evil—who's to blame?
And fold thy hands and acquiesce—Oh,
        shame!
Stand up, speak out, and bravely, in God's
        name!

Be strong!

It matters not how deep intrenched the
        wrong,
How hard the battle goes, the day how long;
Faint not, fight on! To-morrow comes the
        song

—MALTBIE D. BABCOCK

Why should the Great Physician forgive all our sins; heal all our infirmities; save our life from destruction; and complete the gracious work by crowning us with mercy and loving kindness?

What has he in mind *beyond* his healing and redemptive work?

Dr. Maltbie Babcock outlines the answer to this question in the familiar lines of his immortal challenge: "We are not here to play, to dream, to drift! We have hard work to do, and loads to lift!"

The Master would have us ever keep in mind what we are *saved for* as well as what we are *saved from*.

E. H. Sears has wisely said: "To be *dependent on others* for sympathy and comfort makes you weak; to be *self-dependent* makes you weaker still, for that fails you in the day of your greatest need; to become *independent* is a dream of your pride, for no such thing is possible; to become *dependent on God* makes you strong; yea, clothes you out of his own Almightiness, and draws you up into his safety and refuge."

Requiem

Fold thy hands sleeping!
Angels are keeping
   Watch o'er thee now.
See, it is dawning!
Light of the morning
   Falls on thy brow.

White wings are flying!
No more shall dying
   Darken thy day.
Leave thou Death's portal!
Spirit immortal
   Speed on thy way!

When skies are paling
And clouds are sailing
   Over Earth's night,
Only in dreaming
Shall thou be seeming
   Lost to our sight.

Dream mists are drifting!
Fingers are lifting
   Curtains of space!
Framed in its splendor,
Wistful and tender,
   Smiles thy dear face.

—J. WILMER GRESHAM

The souls of the righteous are in the hand of God. This is all we know; all we need to know; all we should really care to know. They are in the hand of God. They share his life; they serve his purposes; they are safe in the keeping of his changeless love.

But our Christian faith draws a step nearer to the shadowy veil that we call death. It tells us that our loved ones are not only safe in God's hand, but it goes far beyond that affirmation. It says that they are increasing in knowledge and love of him; that they are passing from strength to strength in a life of perfect service in his heavenly kingdom; that their lives are ever unfolding in the presence of Christ and in the companionship of saints.

The souls of the righteous are in the hand of God. Yes. But if humanity lives and moves and has its being in God; if we are in the midst of God, like an island in the sea; then the souls of the righteous must be close, very close at hand, impinging upon our conscious thought and feeling, at least in the highest moments of our purest selves, "more present to faith's vision keen than any other vision seen,"—closer than breathing and nearer than hands and feet.

> *"For life is ever Lord of death*
> *And love can never lose its own."*

We will be glad and rejoice. —Isaiah 25:9

A Help to Happiness

Just being happy is a fine thing to do;
Looking on the bright side rather than the blue;
   Sad or sunny musing
   Is largely in the choosing,
And just being happy is brave work and true.

Just being happy helps other souls along;
Their burdens may be heavy and they not strong;
   And your own sky will lighten,
   If others' skies you brighten
By just being happy with a heart full of song.

—RIPLEY D. SAUNDERS

It has been said that there is only one recipe for happiness—make someone else happy, and the little elf of happiness will occupy the guest chamber of memory for many a day.

"Happiness is the natural flower of duty," said Phillips Brooks.

But we must all remember that we cannot pour happiness into a heart any more than we can pour living water into a spring. True happiness must come welling and bubbling up from within.

Said George Macdonald:

"If instead of a gem, or even a flower, we should cast the gift of a loving thought into the heart of a friend, that would be giving, I think, as the angels must give."

Now ye are the body of Christ. —I Cor. 12:27

Jesus Christ and We

Christ has no hands but our hands to do His work
today;
He has no feet but our feet to lead men in His
way;
He has no tongue but our tongue to tell men how
He died;
He has no help but our help to bring them to His
side;
We are the only Bible the careless world will
heed;
We are the sinner's gospel, we are the scoffer's
creed;
We are the Lord's best message given in deed and
word;
What if the type be crooked? What if the print be
blurred?
What if our hands are busy with other work than
His?
What if our feet are walking where sin's allurement
is?
What if our tongues are speaking words His lips
would spurn?
How can we hope to help Him and hasten His
return?

—*ANNIE JOHNSON FLINT*

Is it true—literally true—that "Christ has no other hands than our hands to do his work today"?

That question takes us into the heart of the Incarnation. The Master withdrew from mortal sight promising his unfailing presence in the "beloved community" of his friends until the end of time.

Was he to be a *disembodied Spirit*, flitting to and fro—now here, now there—like some super-angelic Messenger watching over the destinies of the Society he had formed? He seems to have stood in precisely that relation for a fleeting interval following his resurrection. His friends hoped it might continue. They liked the mystic thrill and the *spiritism* of it.

No; he withdrew from human sight that he might be corporately present in the collective consciousness of the group of his followers. They were to be his body—hands and feet and heart and tongue to him.

Love is the fulfilling of the law. —Romans 13:10

The Larger Prayer

At first I prayed for Light;
  Could I but see the way,
How safely, swiftly would I walk
  To everlasting day!

And next I prayed for Strength
  That I might tread the road
With firm, unfaltering feet, and win
  The heaven's serene abode.

And then I asked for Faith;
  Could I but trust my God,
I'd live enfolded in His peace,
  Though foes were all abroad.

But now I pray for Love,
  Deep love to God and man;
A living love that will not fail,
  However dark His plan.

And Light and Strength and Faith
  Are opening everywhere!
God only waited for me till
  I prayed the larger prayer.

—*Edna D. Cheney*

Jacob's vision of a radiant ladder, resting on the solid earth and reaching to the skies, is a symbol of the mounting steps of prayer.

First light; then strength; then faith; then love. These are the angels ascending to the topmost round.

Not until we learn to pray the larger prayer does the revelation come. On the night of the vision the traveler had come to the end of the trail. Would his prayer be answered?

In his dream there were *descending angels*, too. These were the answers to his prayer. When he awoke he could rise upon his feet and go his way, saying, "how holy is this place! This is none other than the House of God. This is the Gate of Heaven!"

The Sanctuary

S oft as the dews of even
  Falling on shadowy sod;
Pure as the breath of Heaven,
  Breathing the life of God;
So, gentle Spirit, come,
  Wooing our souls to rest,
Making our hearts thine home,
  Gracious and tender Guest.

Still as the hush of night,
  Bearing thy gifts of peace;
Fair as the morning light,
  Bidding the darkness cease;
Low at thine altar gate,
  In thy dim temple's shrine,
Silent, on thee we wait,
  Spirit of love divine.

—J. WILMER GRESHAM

We enter through the gates of silence into a consciousness of the presence of God.

It has been said that "silence is beauty; music is beauty. Between the two, man in his little way constantly is trying to express himself. And when he departs a great distance from either, he becomes loud and disagreeable.

Silence is like the sleeping seas. It gathers to itself calmness and strength. It rests upon peace and beauty. It is the whisper of endless Time. It is the purifier of men's souls. It is the mighty force that bears human beings to the realms of greatness."

John Brierly somewhere wrote about the great silent forces that are making our world a better, safer place to live in. The quietly working *physical* forces, gravitation, frost, heat, radio-activity. The *chemical* forces upon which our very existence depends. The *nerve-force* that thrills through the brain of man. The vital forces that lift the flower from its winter grave and send the life-blood to the human heart. The *spiritual* forces, the influence of love and hope and faith—and the unseen Christ. These are the silent forces that are making our world a better, safer place to live in.

A Bedside Prayer

Here is a quiet room!
Pause for a little space;
And in the deepening gloom
With hands before thy face,
Pray for God's grace.

Let no unholy thought
Enter thy musing mind;
Things that the world hath wrought—
Unclean—untrue—unkind—
Leave these behind.

Pray for the strength of God;
Strength to obey His plan;
Rise from your knees less clod
Than when your prayer began,
More of a man.

—DONALD COX

The Bedside Prayer in its spirit and atmosphere suggests the evening blessing of the following familiar lines:

"Sleep meet within this quiet room, O thou whoe'er thou art; nor let sad thoughts of yesterday disturb thy peaceful heart. Nor let tomorrow mar thy rest with thoughts of coming ill; thy Maker is thy changeless Friend—his love surrounds thee still. Forget thyself and all the world; put out each feverish light. The stars are shining overhead, the angels watching o'er thy bed—sleep sweet! Good night! Good nightl!"

O God, who hast drawn over weary day the restful veil of night, wrap our consciences in heavenly peace. Lift from our hands our tasks, and all through the night bear in thy bosom the full weight of our burdens and sorrow, that in untroubled slumber we may press our weakness close to thy strength, and win new power for the morrow's duty from thee, who givest thy beloved sleep.

Ye shall receive power when the Holy Spirit is come upon you. —The Acts 1:8

A Transforming Power

This word power is a favorite in the New Testament. The disciples are endued with power. "The word of the Cross is the power of God." Christ is the "wisdom and the power of God." The phrases are innumerable in which the new revelation of God which comes in Jesus Christ is thought of as coming with power into the world—and the story of that new revelation bears out the promise. Whatever else may be said of Peter and John and Paul and the others whose names greet us in the pages of the New Testament, one fact is perfectly clear: they had been transformed by the power of the Gospel in their lives. Their private interests and their public views had been surrendered to this Jesus Christ whom they called Lord. They had within them a never-failing consciousness of the nearness of God, of an unseen presence, source of power, strength, and vision which they knew as the Holy Spirit or the Spirit of Christ.

—EDWARD L PARSONS

In a little book entitled "What is the Christian Religion?" the thoughtful and scholarly Bishop of California interprets Christianity as a Faith, a Way of Life, a Society, a Transforming Power. The passage on the opposite page considers Christianity as a Transforming Power.

We are reminded of a beloved writer's words about the alchemy of influence. "Since we are what we are by the impacts of those who surround us, those who surround themselves with the highest will be those who change into the highest. *To live with Christ is to make one like Christ.* We all, with unveiled face reflecting as a mirror the glory of Christ, are transformed. into the same image." Wrote Bishop Brent:

"Christ's body was the vehicle of healing power to others. Whoso touched even the hem of his garment with expectation and desire felt the vivifying shocks of imparted physical vitality. When those about him suffered from disease he repaired the disordered mechanism. . . . The body was always and everywhere in his eyes a sacred thing, so sensitively refined that it would be defiled if its possessor harbored an unclean thought or let loose from the lips an unworthy word."

Christ is all and in all. —*Colossians 3:11*

Affirmation

Infinite power of God upholds us,
Infinite love of Christ enfolds us.
Infinite joy within us wells,
Infinite peace within us dwells.
Infinite wisdom guides our way,
Infinite light makes bright our day.
Infinite strength in God we find,
Infinite rest of body and mind.
Infinite life is ours to live,
Infinite thanks to God we give.

—*Ethel P. S. Hoyt*

Profoundly interested in Christian Healing is the author of the "Affirmation of the Infinite" on the opposite page.

The special corner of the field of spiritual healing to which she has devoted her life is the knitting in better mutual understanding and closer co-operation of the leaders of the Christian Healing movement with *medical and mental science*.

God is the only source of health and healing because he is the Author and Giver of *life*.

The *liberation of that life* is through laws and agencies which God has placed either *in our hands* or the *more skilled hands* of those whose human help we seek.

Casting all your care upon Him; for He careth for you.
—1 St. Peter 5:7

The Helper

The little sharp vexations
   And the briars that catch and fret—
Why not take all to the Helper
   Who has never failed us yet?

Tell Him about the heartache,
   And tell Him the longings too,
Tell Him the baffled purpose
   When we scarce know what to do.

Then, leaving all our weakness
   With the One divinely strong,
Forget that we bore the burden,
   And carry away the song.

We have entitled the lines on the opposite page "The Helper." They have been attributed to Phillips Brooks, whose spirit they so truly reflect. They express the grace of Christ—by which we mean his helpfulness.

The grace of Christ is to the moral and spiritual world what the mysterious, ever-present power of healing is in nature.

No *physician ever heals a disease*. All he does is to help nature do her work. Similarly, in the spiritual world, a power of healing—of recuperation—is always at work if we will let it have its own way and work with it.

And that power of *help from the Helper* is as accessible as it is inexhaustible. It is the grace of Christ.

By prayer and supplication with thanksgiving, let your requests be made known unto God. —Philippians 4:6

The Paradox of Prayer

He asked for strength that he might achieve; he was made weak that he might obey.

He asked for health that he might do greater things; he was given infirmity that he might do better things.

He asked for riches that he might be happy; he was given poverty that he might be wise.

He asked for power that he might have the praise of men; he was given weakness that he might feel the need of God.

He asked for all things that he might enjoy life; he was given life that he might enjoy all things.

He has received nothing that he asked for, all that he hoped for. His prayer is answered.

—COL. R. H. FITZHUGH

The story of unanswered prayer lies close to the history of human achievement.

Christ's prayer in the garden, "let this cup pass from me," was unanswered—or answered only in strength given to drink it.

St. Paul's prayer for the removal of the thorn in his side, which was to him as the buffeting of some satanic influence—a thrice-repeated prayer like his Master's—remained unanswered, save for the assurance that the Apostle would have grace to hear it.

Shakespeare wrote—

"We ignorant of ourselves

"Beg oft our own harms, which the wise Powers

"Deny us for our good; so we find profit

"By losing our prayers."

And so the epic of unanswered prayer comes down the Christian centuries.

The prayer of faith always hinges *for its answer* on the higher wisdom and sometimes unrevealed purpose of God.

> *"Prayer is the soul's sincere desire,*
> *Uttered or unexpressed;*
> *The motion of a hidden fire*
> *That trembles in the breast.*
>
> *Prayer is the burden of a sigh,*
> *The falling of a tear,*
> *The upward glancing of an eye,*
> *When none but God is near."*

Behold, I make all things new!
—Revelation 21:5

The Land of Beginning Again

I wish that there were some wonderful place
Called the Land of Beginning Again,
Where all our mistakes and all our heartaches,
And all our poor, selfish grief,
Could be dropped, like a shabby old coat at the door,
And never put on again.

I wish we could come on it all unawares,
Like the hunter who finds a lost trail,
And I wish that the one whom our blindness had
    done
The greatest injustice of all
Could be at the gates, like an old friend that waits,
For the comrade he's gladdest to hail.

We would all find the things we intended to do,
But forgot, and remembered too late,
Like praises unspoken, little promises broken,
And all the thousand and one
Little duties neglected, that might have perfected
The day for one less fortunate.

It wouldn't be possible not to be kind
In the Land of Beginning Again;
And the ones we misjudged, and the ones whom
    we grudged

Their moments of victory here,
Would find in the grasp of our loving handclasp
More than penitent lips could explain.

For what had been hardest we'd know had been best,
And what had seemed loss would be gain;
For there is not a sting that will not take wing,
When we've faced it and laughed it away;
And I think that the laughter is most what we're after,
In the Land of Beginning Again.

—LOUISA P. TARKINGTON

NOTE ON BEGINNING AGAIN

Is the *Land of Beginning Again* a figment of the imagination, a bit of iridescent idealism, a dream from which realism always brings a rude awakening?

Or is it a realm of possibility which we may enter if we only know the secret?

What about the Master's word, "Behold, I make all things new"?

Is not vital Christian experience a land of beginning again?

Of course, for so tremendous a result, *a definite condition* is imposed. We are enjoined to meet the terms of citizenship in the country of our adoption. *"If any man be in Christ Jesus* he is a *new creation*. Old things have passed away! Behold they are become new!"

Come unto Me, all ye that labor and are heavy laden, and I
will give you rest. —St. Matthew 11:28

Rest

Come ye yourselves apart and rest a while,
    Weary, I know it, of the press and throng;
Wipe from your brow the sweat and dust of toil,
And in My quiet strength be strong;

Come ye aside from all the world holds dear,
    For converse which the world has never known;
Alone with Me and with My Father here,
    With Me and with My Father not alone.

Come, tell Me all that ye have said and done,
    Your victories and failures, hopes and fears;
I know how hardy souls are wooed and won,
    My choicest wreaths are always wet with tears.

Come ye and rest! the journey is too great
    And ye will faint beside the way, and sink;
The bread of life is here for you to eat,
    And here for you the wine of love to drink.

Then. fresh from converse with your Lord, return
    And work till daylight softens into even;
The brief hours are not lost in which you learn
    More of your Master and His rest in Heaven.

—*E. H. BICKERSTETH*

We have read that in some parts of India there stand along the road resting-places for those who carry heavy loads upon their heads.

Such a resting-place is called a "Sumatanga."

These rests have a shelf upon which the traveler can easily drop his burden. Beneath is a shady recessed seat where be can quietly rest.

Referring to one of these resting-places, a native Christian woman said, "Christ is my Sumatanga."

Thus Christ himself rested beside the well—the same beloved Master who says to you and to all the fevered ones of earth, "Come unto Me, and I will give you rest."

The Lord shall preserve thy going out and thy coming in.
—Psalm 121:8

An Invocation

The Lord preserve thy going out,
    The Lord preserve thy coming in,
God send His angels round about
    To keep thy soul from every sin.
And when thy going out is done,
    And when thy coming in is o'er,
When in death's darkness all alone,
    Thy feet can come and go no more,
The Lord preserve thy going out
    From this dark world of grief and sin,
While angels standing round about
    Sing "God preserve thy coming in."

The Invocation is at once a salutation and a blessing. It sings itself into our hearts with its quiet rhythm, reminding us of the age-old benediction:

"The Lord bless thee and keep thee;
The Lord make his face to shine upon thee and be gracious unto thee;
The Lord lift up the light of his countenance upon thee and give thee peace!"

The Invocation has about it the quality *of radiance*. Radiance is a vital, elemental quality that comes from *being with the living Christ.* "They looked unto Him, and were radiant." Thus the American Version translates the fifth verse of the 34th Psalm.

We have all known men and women whose lives were radiant with the love of Christ. One could not come near them without feeling a new warmth, a new light, casting a benediction upon the soul.

As Helen Keller wrote, "It is a red-letter day for us when we meet them; they thrill us like a fine poem; their handshake is brimful of unspoken sympathy; their sweet, rich natures impart to our eager, impatient spirits a wonderful restfulness which, in its essence, is divine."

He Leadeth Me

In "pastures green"? Not always; sometimes He
Who knoweth best, in kindness leadeth me
In weary ways, where heavy shadows be.
Out of the sunshine, warm and soft and bright,
Out of the sunshine into darkest night,
I oft would faint with sorrows and affright,
Only for this: I know He holds my hand;
So, whether led in green or desert land,
I trust, although I may not understand.
Beside "still waters"? No, not always so;
Ofttimes the heavy tempests 'round me blow,
And o'er my soul the waves and billows go.
But when the storms beat loudest, and I cry
Aloud for help, the Master standeth by,
And whispers to my soul, "Lo, it is I."
Above the tempest wild I hear Him say:
"Beyond this darkness lies the perfect day;
In every path of thine I lead the way."
So whether on the hilltops high and fair
I dwell, or in the sunless valleys where
The shadows lie, what matter? He is there.
And more than this; Where'er the pathway lead,
He gives to me no helpless, broken reed,
But His own hand, sufficient for my need.

—HENRY H. BARRY

136

The twenty-third Psalm—the song of the Syrian guest—is in the background of the lines on the opposite page. Devotionally that Psalm is to the Old Testament what the Lord's Prayer and the Beatitudes are to the New.

As a companion passage, Christ's description of himself as the Good Shepherd should be read—St. John, Chapter 10.

The words, "Yea, though I walk through the valley of the shadow of death, I will fear no evil; thy rod and Thy staff, they comfort me," are illumined and made reasonable by Christ's own experience of the "valley of the shadow."

> *He is a Path, if any be misled,*
> *He is a robe, if any naked He;*
> *If any chance to hunger, He is bread;*
> *It any be a bondman, He is free;*
> *It any be but weak, how strong is He!*
> *To dead men life He is, to sick men health,*
> *To blind the sight, and to the needy, wealth—*
> *A pleasure without loss, a treasure without stealth."*

Be glad in the Lord, and rejoice, ye righteous.
—Psalm 32:11

Laughter

A laugh is just like sunshine,
It freshens all the day,
It tips the peak of life with light
And drives the clouds away.
The soul grows glad that hears it,
And feels its courage strong.
A laugh is just like sunshine
For cheering folks along.

A laugh is just like music,
It lingers in the heart,
And where its melody is heard,
The ills of Life depart;
And happy thoughts come crowding
Its joyful note to greet—
A laugh is just like music
For making living sweet.

—R. D. Saunders

NOTE ON SMILES

In the vestibule of a certain hospital, visitors see a card bearing this advice:

"Never utter a discouraging word while you are in this hospital. You should come here only for the purpose of helping. Keep your hindering, sad looks for other places. *If you can't smile, don't go in.*"

"If you can't smile, don't go in!"

It is good advice for others besides hospital visitors. Who is beyond the ministry of a kindly, sunny smile?

Let us learn by heart Margaret Bailey's lines:

> *God, give me sympathy and sense,*
> *And help me keep my courage high;*
> *God, give me calm and confidence,*
> *And—please—a twinkle in my eye.*

The prayers of the saints ascended up before God.
—Revelation 8:4

Intercession

For friends above; for friends still left below;
For the rare links invisible between;
For Thine unsearchable greatness; for the veils
Between us and the things we may not know;
For those high times when hearts take wings and
      rise,
And float secure above earth's mysteries;
For that wide, open avenue of prayer,
All radiant with Thy glorious promises;
For sweet hearts tuned to noblest Charity;
For great hearts toiling in the outer dark;
For friendly hands stretched out in time of need;
For every gracious thought and word and
      deed,—
    We thank Thee, Lord!

—John Oxenham

The thought in the lines on the opposite page is a very precious one.

Friend prays for friend *here*. Why should death block the channel of intercession?

Why should not we speak to God for those we knew and loved while here? And if that be so, *why may not they speak to him for us*, knowing as they do our fiercest struggles and our deepest needs?

For aught we know they may be the appointed guardians of our life. We want no ministering angels who are strangers to our lives. Back of the proffer of the helping hand, whether human or divine, we want the understanding heart of those who knew and loved us here.

LOVE
to Guide Our Journey

The Bridge Builder

A pilgrim, going a lone highway,
Came at evening, cold and gray,
  To a chasm, deep and vast and wide.
  The old man crossed in the twilight dim.
  The chasm held no fears for him.
  But he paused when be reached the other side
  And built a bridge to span the tide.
  "Old man," said a fellow pilgrim near,
  "Why waste your time in building here?
  Your journey ends with the close of day,
  You never again will pass this way.
  You've crossed the chasm deep and wide.
  Why build ye here at eventide?"
  The pilgrim raised his old grey head,
  "My friend, in the path I've come," he said,
  "There followeth after me today
  A fair-haired youth who must pass this way.
  The chasm which held no fear for me
  To the fair-haired youth may a pitfall be.
  He, too, must cross in the twilight dim.
  My friend, I am building this bridge for him."

—WILL ALLEN DROMGOOLE

It is not enough that we should have spanned the chasm of life with the bridge of our own personal achievement. *Only the bridges of our failure may we burn behind us.*

The trails of success that we have blazed belong to those who follow. Even the saving of our souls is unworthy as an end in itself. Nay, it is impossible as an end in itself. Did not the Master say that he that would save his soul must lose it in the larger service of mankind?

"He saved others, himself he cannot save!" This was meant as a taunt. It was in fact the highest tribute of the cross.

The Summit

Why speak of those whom age is crowning
As "going slowly *down* the hill,"
When on the heights above them shining
Stands one who beckons *upwards* still?

No sad descent to death and darkness
Is life when lived with Love as Guide;
But ever climbing towards the hilltop
Each summit gained brings visions wide.

'Tis always up the Pilgrims travel;
Whilst Love rejoices, at their side,
To feel the press of faith more strongly,
To know He's near, whate'er betide.

As Love the Pilgrims forward leadeth
Footsteps may falter, eyes grow dim,
But every sigh He quickly heareth
And not a pain is hid from Him.

The steepest crags lie all behind them:
By gentle slopes He guides the way:
Then one last step—still up—He bears them,
To find the joy of perfect day.

—*M. H.*

Somewhere near the snowy summit of the Alps there is an inscription that marks the last resting place of an Alpine guide. Just three short words tell the story: "He died climbing."

We often hear it said that such an one is "growing old." But as a matter of fact we do not *grow* old. We only *get old* when we *cease to grow*—and climb.

Youth is essentially of the spirit, not of the calendar. To have made the climb of life is to have proved that while "winter may be on the head, eternal youth is still within the heart."

We may be sixty, or seventy, or eighty *years young*.

"Lord, plant my spirit high upon the crest
of Thine eternal strength!
Then, though life's breaking struggles come at length,
Their storms shall only bend me to Thy breast."

Bear ye one another's burdens, and so fulfill the law of Christ.
—Galations 6:2

Friendship

I would be true, for there are those who trust me;
I would be pure, for there are those that care.
I would be strong, for there is much to suffer;
I would be brave, for there is much to dare.
I would be friend of all, the foe, the friendless;
I would be giving, and forget the gift.
I would be humble, for I know my weakness;
I would look up—and laugh—and love—and lift.

—HOWARD ARNOLD WALTER

Truth, honor, faith, trust, love, these are links in the chain of friendship.

Friendship is forever re-incarnating its pure spirit. It is, therefore, forever young and forever beautiful.

Whenever the rebirth of friendship happens the angels sing and the star shines over the dusty fields of life, just as when the Christ-child came.

For many years we have kept among our treasures these precious words of Charles Kingsley on friendship:

"A blessed thing it is for any man or woman to have a friend, one human soul whom we can trust, whom we can trust utterly, who knows the best and worst of us, and who loves us in spite of our faults; who will speak the honest truth to us. while the world flatters us to our face, and laughs at us behind our back; who will give as counsel and reproof in the days of prosperity and self conceit, but who, again will comfort and encourage us in the days of difficulty and sorrow, when the world leaves us alone to fight our battles as we can."

Lord, Thou knowest that I love Thee. —St. John 21:16

In Silence

L ord, I have no words to say
    My love to Thee—
I lean my cheek against Thy hand
    Quite silently,
And know that Thou wilt see into
    The heart of me.

Lord, I cannot sing great hymns
    Of praise to Thee—
But into Thine, I slip my hand,
    All silently
And give, for Thee to guard and keep,
    The soul of me.

—*Lucy A. K. Adee*

It was Wordsworth who wrote, "to me the meanest flower that blows can give thoughts that do often lie too deep for tears."

There are emotions that come to every heart that lie too deep for *words*.

The tiny poem on the opposite page, "Lord, I have no words to say my love to Thee—I lean my cheek against Thy hand quite silently," is illustrative of the utter inadequacy of language to convey the deeper feelings of the heart.

Out of the unsyllabled silence—and the upward look of the soul—may come the whispered accents of prayer. Sara Nichols Guild has caught the spirit of this mood. Her simple lines tell us that our fellowship with God in prayer may be voiced or unexpressed.

> *Prayer is so simple;*
> *It is like quietly opening a door*
> *And slipping into the very Presence of God,*
> *There in the stillness*
> *To listen for His voice.*
> *Perhaps to petition,*
> *Or only to listen;*
> *It matters not;*
> *Just to be there,*
> *In His Presence,*
> *Is prayer!*

The eternal God is thy refuge, and underneath are the
everlasting arms. —Deuteronomy 33:27

The Everlasting Arms

All this week I am going to live worthily as a child of God. His love is round me. Underneath are the Everlasting Arms. I am going to be honest and true, and brave in all the events of life, and I believe that to those who love God all things work together for good. I am going to rise above all worry, fretting, fear, and hatred, to live in an atmosphere of spiritual serenity. My life is part of God's plan, and that which is divine within me can never fail nor be defeated. Behind all that comes, God's love and wisdom will be present to strengthen and sustain.

—ALBERT N. PALMER

NOTE ON "THE EVERLASTING ARMS"

Some familiar "Affirmations of the Spirit" have been considered in earlier pages of "Wings." Here we find ourselves musing upon another spiritual affirmation, "The Everlasting Arms."

It is in the spirit of the Ninety-first Psalm, which should be read as a parallel reading. The fifth verse of that Psalm begins with what has sometimes been called *The eleventh commandment*, "Thou shall not be afraid."

Let us remember as we make our affirmation that the Protecting Arms are *around others* as truly as around ourselves, and that in the midst of the Fellowship of Affirmation stands the Master himself.

Be ye transformed by the renewing of your mind.
—Romans 12:2

What Spiritual Healing Does

Gradually an inner peace and tranquillity came to me in so positive a way that my manner changed greatly. My children and friends commented upon it. All feelings of irritability disappeared. Even the expression of my face changed noticeably.

I had been bigoted, aggressive, and intolerant. . . . I grew broadly tolerant toward the views of others. I had been nervous and irritable, coming home two or three times a week with a sick headache induced, as I then supposed, by dyspepsia and catarrh. I grew serene and gentle, and the physical troubles entirely disappeared. I had been in the habit of approaching every business interview with an almost morbid fear. I now meet every one with confidence and inner calm.

I may say that the growth has all been toward the elimination of selfishness . . . it has been in the direction of a practical, working realization of the immanence of God and the divinity of man's true inner self.

NOTE ON WHAT SPIRITUAL HEALING DOES

Healing testimonies rise in the scale of value according to the character of those who offer them. William James writes in measured words of what spiritual healing meant to him. He will be remembered as the founder of the modern school of *pragmatic* philosophy. Pragmatism tests the truth of a principle by its results.

Spiritual healing begins with the inner self. It first utters the ancient cry of the soul, "Make me a *clean heart*, O God, and renew a *right spirit* within me."

As it moves from the spiritual center to the physical circumference of our being it guides the currents of our thinking and directs the stream of our emotional nature.

Peace comes to the troubled mind, rest to the jangled nerves; and *power is released through poise.*

As a result of this process new sources of life are tapped for body and soul.

Is not this what the Apostle means when he says, "He that raised up Christ from the dead shall also vitalize your dying bodies by his spirit that dwelleth in you"? (Romans 8:11.)

There standeth One in your midst.
—St. John 1:26.

The Presence of Christ

Consider what our lives would be, if through an active cooperation with our Lord we were faithful to our mysterious possession of him—what an unfolding of wondrous light in thought, in word, in deed, in aspiration, in design, would characterize our inward nature!

What an upholding Strength would sustain us, what a Companionship be felt within, what communing with our unseen Guest, if only we could always bear in mind what it is to receive God; could think and feel and act in conformity with the conviction of his Indwelling Presence, possessing and possessed, though hidden under an inscrutable veil, screened from all mortal sense!

—T. T. Carter

Every spiritual truth is wedded to its companion duty. Because God has revealed himself to man certain momentous consequences follow. Man's spiritual *life-line* runs in a single unmistakable direction. God's voice, God's presence, God's movements, must be traced in every incident as well as in the totality of human experience.

God's final word to man is Christ. Christ expresses all that can be humanly known of God. And Christ's central and supreme promise, to which all his other promises stand related, and in which they find their meaning, is that of his abiding presence all the days, even unto the consummation of time.

> *The night was long; the shadows spread*
> *As far as the eye could see.*
> *I stretched my hand to a human Christ,*
> *And he walked through the dark with me.*
> *Out of the dimness at last we came,*
> > *Our feet on the dawn-warmed sod,*
> *And I saw by the light in his wondrous eye,*
> *I walked with the Son of God.*

In due season we shall reap if we faint not.
—Galations 6:9

Life and Work

While we work there's chance for giving;
While we give life's worth the living;
While we live there's room for growing;
While we grow there's time for sowing.
Watchful care and faithful keeping,
When we've sown there's hope for reaping.

—RUTH ROYCE

To write a note on "Life and Work" is to recall the life and work of Ruth Royce, and to be grateful for her gifts of mind and heart. Nor can we forget her careful reading of the earliest edition of the *Wings*, when the little book, now so widely known, had not yet appeared.

Her brother, Josiah Royce of Harvard, has been "guide, philosopher, and friend," to hosts of men and women of our generation, and is numbered among the immortals of the nation.

We link their memories in this tribute.

> *I shall pass through*
> *This world but once.*
> *Any good thing*
> *Therefore I can do,*
> *Or any kindness that I*
> *Can show to any human being,*
> *Let me do it now—*
> *Let me not defer it—*
> *Nor neglect it, for*
> *I shall not pass this way again.*

The greatest of these is love. —I Cor. 13:13

The Golden Key

One by one the earliest friends of Jesus, as they relayed the glad tidings of the angels, came to their Master's position that love is the key of all life, human and divine. The key of love was turned in the lock of the being of God. And it fitted so perfectly that they went forth and told men that God was their Father—that they, as truly as the Lord Christ, are sons of God—that they, as truly as the Man of Galilee, might grow into his spiritual image. The problem of duty was unlocked with the same key. Love was found to be the fulfilling of every duty, small and great. Even the ancient mystery of death yielded to the magic key of love. Is it not true that the eye of faith, as it peers wistfully through that shadowy veil, beholds unbroken the sceptered sway of love?

—J. WILMER GRESHAM

A recent writer discusses the question, "What was the greatest word of Christ?"

We are accustomed to say that the Master's greatest word was *love*. "Love," we are told, "is the greatest thing in the world."

But was not Christ's greatest word *life*, rather than love? Must we not live before we can love; and is not God the living God before he is the loving God?

But the fact still stands that only the key of love can unlock the meaning of life.

If love without life is impossible, life without love is unintelligible.

> *The night has a thousand eyes,*
> *The day but one;*
> *Yet the light of the bright world dies*
> *With the dying sun.*
>
> *The mind has a thousand eyes,*
> *And the heart but one;*
> *Yet the light of a whole life dies*
> *When love is done.*

—FRANCIS W. BOURDILLON.

God is love; and he that dwelleth in love dwelleth in God,
and God in him. —1 John 4:16

The Cost of Love

If love should count you worthy, and should deign
One day to seek your door and be your guest,
Pause! ere you draw the bolt and bid him rest,
If in your old content you would remain;
For not alone he enters; in his train
Are angels of the mist; the lonely quest;
Dreams of the unfulfilled and unpossessed;
And sorrow, and life's immemorial pain.
He wakes desires you never may forget,
He shows you stars you never saw before,
He makes you share with him forevermore
The burden of the world's divine regret.
How wise you were to open not! and yet
How poor if you should turn him from the door!

—S. R. LYSAGHT

Much has been written about love as the supreme gift. Have you ever paused to consider the cost of love? Strange and even paradoxical as it may seem, love, the most priceless *gift* in the universe, is *costly* beyond the willingness of the human heart to possess it.

But, you ask if love is a *gift*, why speak of it in terms of *cost* to ourselves?

This is the theme of Lysaght's unforgettable lines in this exquisite sonnet from "Poems of the Unknown Way." If we ask of love, "what are these wounds in thine hands?" love replies "these are the wounds wherewith I have been wounded in the house of my friends." Love is hourly wounded by surface sentiment and unworthy sentimentality—the weapons of so-called friends who covet the *gift* but fain would evade the *cost*.

In love's train are "angels of the mist, the lonely quest, dreams of the unfulfilled and unpossessed—and sorrow." The gift is costly. But let love's footfalls at the threshold sound ever so lightly, and lo, the hour of the soul strikes. How wise to open not. Yet how poor to turn him from the door!

> "Life has no other logic
>   And time no other creed
> Than: *I for joy will follow*
>   *Where thou for love dost lead.*"

Proof

I f radio's slim fingers
  Can pluck a melody
From night, and toss it over
  A continent or sea;

If the petalled white notes
  Of a violin
Are blown across a mountain
  Or a city's din;

If songs, like crimson roses,
  Are culled from the thin blue air,
Why should mortals wonder
  If God hears prayer?

—Ethel Romig Fuller

NOTE ON "PROOF"

Today with radio *inaudible things may be clearly heard.* Tomorrow with television *invisible things may be clearly seen.*

No thoughtful person can tune in and hear the clear and natural tones of a human voice thousands of miles away without musing upon the silent world of spirit.

Out of the silences *God may be signaling us.* We must know his wavelengths. Out of the silences *friends in the spirit world* may be awaiting a turn of our dial. We must improve our selectivity.

The exquisite poem "Proof" first appeared in Sunset Magazine. It is from the pen of Ethel Romig Fuller. In a letter the writer expresses her happiness at its inclusion here.

Behold I stand at the door and knock. —Revelation 3:20

At the Door

Today Christ may be standing at the door of your life. The strong, vital, imperial Christ may be standing there. You have been told that it is an easy thing to push the bolt and let him in. It is not an easy thing. It is the supremest thing in all the world. And because it is the supremest thing it is the hardest thing.

But before inviting Christ to be your house guest, why not make a survey of your mental house? Think of the permanent guests that are already there. Think, if you will, of the houseguests that are spending not the holidays only, not the weekend only, but all the time, uninvited and unwelcome though many of them be.

He it is who waits upon the threshold of your life today. He it is who knocks. Knocks gently in sorrow. Knocks tenderly in grief. Knocks sweetly in joy. Knocks firmly in sin.

And because he gives all he demands all.

—J. Wilmer Gresham

The house of personality is built of many stories. There are the shining upper stories of the *superconscious* mind. There are the shadowy lower stories of the *subconscious* self. And there are many rooms and many doors. Christ stands upon the threshold of the *conscious* mind. We hear his voice, and bid him enter and abide. We show him into the guest room of the soul.

Then one day he says, 'There is one room in your house I have never entered. When I pass the door it is always shut. Do let me see it."

Perhaps it is the room where certain desires are stored away that we will not forsake. Perhaps it is where we keep an old hatred or a secret grudge. Perhaps it is whre we cherish a shameful hope, or where some idolatry sits enthroned.

Then, as we sit in our chamber of meditation, a revealing thought comes to us. It is this. *Christ offers his whole self to our whole selves.*

Little Things

Oh, it's just the little homely things,
The unobtrusive, friendly things,
The "Won't-you-let-me-help-you" things,
That make our pathway light.

And it's just the jolly, joking things,
The "Never-mind-the-trouble" things,
The "Laugh-with-me-it's-funny" things,
That make the world seem bright,

For all the countless famous things,
The wondrous record-breaking things,
Those never-to-be-equaled things,
That all the papers cite

Are not like the little human things,
The every-day-encountered things,
The "Just-because-I-like-you" things,
That make us happy quite.

Happiness has been defined as "doing good by stealth and having it found out by accident." But that makes happiness too self-conscious—just a bit artificial. Also it becomes a fleeting emotion.

Aristotle comes closer when he speaks of happiness as "an energizing of the soul in accordance with virtue." We might put it in our own way and think of happiness as *a sense of kinship with the divine and a service of the ideal in all the happenings of daily living.*

The kingdom of happiness is always at hand, closely at hand. It is the unconscious reaction of our spirits to "little, nameless, unremembered acts of kindness and of love."

Because of Thee

L ord of my life, I shall ever try to keep my body pure, knowing that Thy loving touch is upon all my limbs.

I shall ever try to keep all untruths out from my thoughts, knowing that Thou art that truth which has kindled the light of reason in my mind.

I shall ever try to drive all evils away from my heart and keep my love in flower, knowing that Thou hast Thy seat in the inmost shrine of my heart.

And it shall be my endeavor to reveal Thee in my actions, knowing it is Thy power gives one strength to act.

—RABINDRANATH TAGORE

Motives give color to deeds. Deeds in turn give visibility to motives.

In this mystic meditation of Tagore we note *the motive to purity*. It is that the Lord hath placed his touch upon our limbs. We also note *the motive to truth*. He hath kindled the light of reason in our minds, and *the motive to love*. He hath placed his seat in the inmost shrine of our heart.

The poet is intrigued by beauty. But he looks *beyond beauty*, which is caught like a point of light in the soul, *to God*. God, the eternal one, is fadeless beauty, ultimate reality, uncreated love.

This thought runs close to the teaching of the Master. Christ bade men follow the line of purity, of truth, of love, to the end that they might be *like God*, or—as he put it—the children of their Father in heaven.

Ye are my friends. —St. John 15:14

From Johanan, Collector at Magdala, to Zacchæus, Commissioner of Taxes at Jericho.
(Part One)

M y Dear Zacchæus:

I have had Jesus the prophet of Nazareth to dinner today and a number of our friends came to meet him. I promised to let you know what happened, but I promised too much. I will tell you what I can, but it is only an hour since he went, and he has left me full of thoughts. As you know, I was rather nervous about the whole affair. First thing this morning I would have given a good deal to stop the dinner altogether. You and I often say that our sort of people are no worse than other folk, but when I went over the invitations in my mind, I couldn't help feeling that we were queer company for such a man as Jesus. I wondered what would happen if Reuben began talking the way he does sometimes, and I meant to give him a hint before the meal began. However, I did not get an opportunity, and as it happened there was no need. Reuben wasn't himself today.

FIRST NOTE ON "JOHANAN'S LETTER"

This letter of Johanan to Zacchæus is not only a creation of great literary beauty. It is equally an achievement of deep spiritual insight.

For many years we wondered who wrote it. Now we know that it is the work of Dr. W. Russell Maltby, Warden of the Deaconess Order at Ilkley, England. We deeply value his kind note, consenting to its inclusion here.

Schiller says "you can tell an artist by what he leaves out. He does not crowd everything into his picture. He chooses a central figure and subordinates everything else to it."

The central figure in the letter of Johanan is vividly drawn. It is unmistakably that of the gracious Master of men. There are other figures in the scene, Benjamin, Rachel and the rest, but they draw their light from the Radiant One whose glory rests on all.

They took knowledge of them that they had been with Jesus.
—The Acts 4:13

From Johanan to Zacchæus
(Part Two)

W ell, Jesus came. What is he like? If you had asked me halfway through the dinner, I should have said that he was the nicest man I had ever met. But now I think,—oh, I don't know what I think, except that I am not fit to touch his feet. Of course, we were all very anxious to hear him talk. Reuben was hoping that he would give the Pharisees a dressing down, and made an opening for him. But Jesus never mentioned the Pharisees, and to tell the truth I believe we all forgot that there were such people. He seemed just as ready to listen as to talk. And what a listener he is! I never met anyone who listens as he does. I happened to mention my boy Benjamin, for we are wondering what trade to put him to, and of course we are rather anxious as there are not many openings for a publican's son. Jesus was interested immediately, and asked me questions about the lad. He told me something too about his own boyhood. I began to feel rather ashamed at last, for you know it is very strange to meet some one who understands your own lad better than you do yourself. But he does understand boys.

I cannot tell you all the things we talked about. They were much the same kind of things you and I might speak of, but there was a difference. I found myself talking to him as though I had known him all my life.

The second part of the letter closes with a confession, a revealing confession. "I cannot tell you all the things we talked about. They were much the same kind of things you and I might speak of, but there was a *difference*. I found myself talking to him as though I had known him all my life."

This is just what happened in the *recorded* conversations of Jesus throughout his ministry.

The woman at the well, Nicodemus, the disciples, all who talked with him, had the same reaction. Seeming trivialities were little gates through which he led them into wider fields of understanding.

The Master's gift of insight became their own. It spoke to them of "a nobleness that lies in others, sleeping but never dead." Men and women came to detect a *difference* in their talk, their expressions, their deeds. They took knowledge of them that they had been with Jesus.

When He shall appear we shall be like Him. —I John 3:2

From Johanan to Zacchæus
(Part Three)

I began telling him—I can't think how I did it—how I got into this business of ours, and I was explaining our difficulties and how impossible it is always to keep straight when everyone is trying to take advantage of you, especially in these hard times when the future is so uncertain and one must make provision while one can for wife and family. He just listened, and looked straight in my face as though he understood all I said—and all I didn't say as well—and as though he were sorry for us. He didn't interrupt, or argue with me, but the more I looked at him, the more I wished I had never got into the cursed business and the more I wished I could begin again.

You will think it ridiculous, but as he sat there, I wondered why we were not all like him. We were all sick, and he alone was well. I remembered the time when you and I were boys together, and I felt that we had missed the road. If I had been alone with him, I think I should have made a clean breast of it, and asked him what to do. He could see that my feelings were getting out of hand,—they say in the town that Johanan has no feelings, and I half believed them until today. But really the tears were in my eyes, and I had such a longing, and felt so helpless. And Jesus said to me, as though he understood everything, "Don't be afraid. Think it over again, and remember your heavenly Father knows what you need. Don't lose your life in trying to save it." Do you see what he meant?

"Jesus was a wonderful companion, always quick to sympathize, always ready to listen. He had that spiritual sense of touch that we call tact, that gift of suddenly finding the point of contact with all sorts of people."

Here in this third part of the letter of Johanan we find Jesus as a Master of the art of *creative listening*. Johanan says that Jesus listened "as though he understood all that he (Johanan) said, and all that he didn't say as well."

We may believe that as the Master listened he saw back of each speaker the man or woman he would have each to be. Then, when pauses in the conversation came, he was able to speak constructively, leading on and up "until with unveiled face" they came to reflect the pure and perfect image of the Father in whose likeness all were made.

Christ's secret is an open secret to his real friends.

*The Son of man is come to seek and to save that
which was lost.* —St. Luke 19:10

From Johanan to Zacchæus
(Part Four)

Well, the meal ended, and I was bidding him goodbye at the door, when the girl Rachel— perhaps you guess her trade—came up to the door, and I felt the blood rush to my cheeks, lest she should show that she knew me. But she had eyes only for Jesus. Some of his friends drew back when they saw her, but Jesus himself gave her a look which I shall never forget, went straight up to her, and said only this, "Don't do it any more." She stood gazing after him as he went, then covered her face with her hands, and ran down the street. As for me, I watched him till he was out of sight, and had hard work not to run after him. He is on his way to Jerusalem, and is to pass through Jericho. I mentioned you to him. Be sure you see him. Don't let anything stop you.

Peace be with you.

P. S. Benjamin has just come in. You would love that boy, Zacchæus. I must be a better father to him. Do you remember the first time you and I went up to the temple? We were Benjamin's age. Do you remember how we all sang as we went up—

Who shall ascend into the hill of the Lord?
He that hath clean hands and a pure heart.

We have missed our way, Zacchæus. But I think since Jesus was here, that God has not altogether cast us off. Do you think we could begin again?

Sometimes a little postscript sums up in a few lines the heart of the letter to which it is appended.

Note the closing sentence of the letter of Johanan. "We have missed our way, Zacchæus. But I think, since Jesus was here, that God has not altogether cast us off. Do you think we could begin again?"

"Life is full of vicious circles," wrote Lucy Jenkins in that helpful book, *In His Presence*. "Take your circle and break it and twist it into a spiral, a *never-ending spiral* and climb forever upward in your ceaseless search for higher and higher forms of self-expression, for Truth, and God."

It shall come to pass that at evening time it shall be light.
—Zechariah 14:7

A Prayer for Each Day

Let me do my work each day; and if the darkened hours of despair overcome me, may I not forget the strength that comforted me in the desolation of other times. May I still remember the bright hours that found me walking over the silent hills of my childhood, or dreaming on the margin of the quiet river, when a light glowed within me, and I promised my early God to have courage amid the tempests of the changing years.

Spare me from bitterness and from the sharp passions of unguarded moments. May I not forget that poverty and riches are of the spirit. Though the world know me not, may my thoughts and actions be such as shall keep me friendly with myself. Lift my eyes from the earth, and let me not forget the uses of the stars. Forbid that I should judge others lest I condemn myself.

Let me not follow the clamor of the world, but walk calmly in my path. Give me a few friends, who will love me for what I am; and keep ever burning before my vagrant steps the kindly light of hope. And though age and infirmity overtake me, and I come not within sight of the castle of my dreams, teach me still to be thankful for life, and for time's olden memories that are good and sweet; and may the evening's twilight find me gentle still.

—MAX ERDMAN

NOTE ON THE DAY'S PRAYER

With Max Erdman's Prayer for Each Day—a tenderly personal prayer—we bring the Wings of Healing nearly to a close.

The writer of the Apocalypse speaks of "golden bowls, full of incense, which are the *prayers* of the saints." The golden bowl is the visible *form* of the saintly prayer; the wreathing cloud of incense is the *spirit*.

This is true of the "Prayer for Each Day." It is exquisite *in form* and *noble in inspiration*.

Needless to add that the spirit of healing pervades its aspirations as it moves like a quiet river through the land of memory.

Though it tarry, wait for it; because it will surely come, it will not tarry. —Hab. 2:3.

Waiting By the Pool

Today, as in the days of old, the Master would heal in soul and body all who come to him with faith in his power to heal. But there are many sufferers, who, believing in the power of Christ to heal—and having come to him for healing—*yet remain unhealed.* They still suffer from pain and weariness of body. They are still held in bondage by sickness and disease of soul. They are like the throng of sufferers at the Pool of Bethesda. "They are watching for the moving of the waters. They are *waiting at the pool.*

Let those who are waiting at the pool take heart. All of us who in simple faith have come to Christ for healing—even though we have waited through long, patient years for the moving of the waters—are in a *stage* of being healed. A crisis took place in our lives when we came to him. And we may never have wavered, even in hours of intense bodily pain. Now we know that something happened within us in that great moment of the soul. And we believe more firmly than ever that the Master is in the vestibule of the temple of healing and will soon be bending over us with all power in heaven and earth to heal.

Some of us may enter the light sooner than others. *But we are all moving towards it.* A train in a tunnel does not bring each passenger at the same time out of darkness into the light of day. Those in the front part of the train are the first to see the glimmer of light.

They leave the tunnel behind while their fellow passengers are still in the dark. But even while the train is in the tunnel all are moving towards the light. So all who have started on the journey towards health of body and soul will reach their destination.

—BY ONE STILL WAITING BY THE POOL.

NOTE ON WAITING BY THE POOL

There are different kinds of waiting. There is *passive* waiting that becomes dispirited when the cherished object of desire seems remote of accomplishment. "Hope deferred maketh the heart sick." Passive waiting is a lamp whose flame if untended will flicker and die. Then, if the object of our waiting should eventually come, it would find us unprepared for its fulfillment.

But there is another kind of waiting. It is *expectant* waiting. Expectant waiting differs from passive waiting in its *vital* quality. It endures, not as a gesture of resignation, but "as seeing him who is invisible." Hours may slip into days, and days into weeks and months and years, but its fire burns all the brighter. Why? Because its embers are fanned by a living spirit that reinforces the human spirit from within.

Are you "waiting at the pool," seemingly alone, friendless, while many another whose need is not so great as yours has heard the murmur and seen the movement of the healing waters? Then remember that the Master himself is also waiting by the pool, *waiting for you* there. And his waiting glows with a divine expectancy. The time for your perfect healing is in his keeping. Yes. But in yours also.

May the hands of the Great Physician
of soul and body
fold the Wings of Healing over
each troubled heart.